BLACK AMERICANS IN MOURNING

Black Americans in Mourning

*Reactions to the Assassination
of Abraham Lincoln*

Leonne M. Hudson

SOUTHERN ILLINOIS UNIVERSITY PRESS

CARBONDALE

Southern Illinois University Press
www.siupress.com

Printed in the United States of America
First printed July 2024.

Cover illustration: Civil War veteran James Brown of Illinois
at age 104 showing his admiration for Abraham Lincoln.
Collection of the Smithsonian National Museum of African American
History and Culture, Gift from the Liljenquist Family Collection.

ISBN 978-0-8093-3972-3 (cloth)
ISBN 978-0-8093-3954-9 (paperback)
ISBN 978-0-8093-3955-6 (ebook)

This book has been catalogued with the Library of Congress.

Printed on recycled paper ♻

SIU
Southern Illinois University System

This book is dedicated
to
Cassandra and Evan

CONTENTS

ILLUSTRATIONS

PREFACE

My visit to Abraham Lincoln's birthplace in Hardin County, Kentucky, several years ago sparked my interest to pursue a study of the man who would become the sixteenth president of the nation and one of the most influential figures in world history. My challenge was to come up with an aspect of his life that had not been comprehensively explored in the more than sixteen thousand works about him. It is safe to say that Lincoln as a person, politician, and president has been examined by historians and scholars in one form or another since his death nearly 160 years ago. At no time did I consider a biographical work about him. After a great deal of thought, I settled on the topic of African Americans' reactions to his death. After the selection, I was still not convinced that I wanted to undertake such a study. Years went by, and then I had a conversation with John T. Hubbell, my colleague at Kent State University. He encouraged me to pursue the topic. I took his advice and went to work on producing the current monograph. I am indebted to him for his unwavering support throughout this process. I also appreciate the fact that he would contact me periodically to check on my progress and to offer suggestions for improving the book.

The research for this project took me to many libraries and archival depositories between Illinois and Louisiana, including the National Archives and the Library of Congress. I traveled sometimes by plane but most often by car in search of sources that would help to tell the story of the response of Black people to the assassination. At times it appeared that the trips would never end. One more depository in one more town or city. When I unearthed a letter, diary, journal, or correspondence that was pertinent to my topic, I knew that the effort was worth the investment. This study has been enriched by the sources found in the various depositories across the country.

In addition to the church, African American periodicals were one of the most important cultural institutions in the Black community. Their editors and reporters spoke out against racism while advocating for equality among the races. Newspapers, especially Black journals, proved indispensable in telling the story of how African Americans dealt with the unexpected news of the assassination. The *Christian Recorder*, the official newspaper of the African Methodist Episcopal Church, headquartered in Philadelphia, was especially helpful. It contained a wealth of information pertinent to this study. This source was rich with editorials, as well as letters from ordinary men and women, influential religious and political leaders, and soldiers. The *Weekly-Anglo African* (New York), the *Black Republican* (New Orleans), the *New Orleans Tribune*, and the *Elevator* (San Francisco) were also extremely valuable to this work. Although numerous formerly enslaved people were not literate, many were able to document their reflections in their own vernacular or through others.

Recording why and how African Americans mourned the death of Lincoln reveals a portrait of a crestfallen race. One of the most enduring consequences of the Civil War was the liberation of millions of enslaved people, which guaranteed that Lincoln's legacy and reputation would be "inextricably linked" to people of color for generations.[1] Many Blacks believed that a small piece of their lives had died along with the president. Although his personal interaction with Black Americans was limited, that did not diminish their sorrow for him. By the time Lincoln had been entombed at Oak Ridge Cemetery in May 1865, hundreds of thousands of Americans of both races had participated in his funeral. This book conveys the authenticity of the emotional outpourings of people of color at a time when their hearts were heavy-laden.

This record of their responses to the assassination fills a void in the history of our nation's greatest president. It captures the sentiments of a cross-section of the Black population. To allow the reader to fully appreciate the sincerity of African Americans, the book examines the words they wrote and spoke as close as possible to the assassination itself. Chronicling the reactions of people of color to the assassination of Abraham Lincoln was a demanding but enjoyable journey.

ACKNOWLEDGMENTS

Historians do not complete their projects without incurring many debts along the way. After years of researching and writing, the time has come to recognize those people and institutions that helped me to bring this study to a successful conclusion. I would like to start by thanking Carolyn Brothers, who motivated me with words of encouragement when finishing this project seemed insurmountable. I am grateful to Zachery Fry, Claire Lucas, Miranda K. Shield, and Cora Slack, who provided me with useful information at various times. I would like to extend a thank-you to Jennifer Hivick, who located some sources for the book. I am grateful to Julie A. Mujic for her support and encouragement during this undertaking. I thank Judith Bosau-Allen, who graciously read the work and provided helpful comments. I extend heartfelt gratitude to the external readers. Jonathan W. White and the anonymous readers provided invaluable suggestions that enhanced the quality of the book.

I owe a debt of gratitude to Kelly D. Mezurek for unearthing sources that helped to tell the story of how Black Americans reacted to Abraham Lincoln's assassination, especially United States Colored Troops. She read the manuscript at an early stage and provided valuable comments for improving it. Kelly always seemed to know when to contact me with a reminder to keep pressing forward. Her motivation inspired me to see the project through.

Kent State University was supportive of this effort. I am happy to recognize the Department of History, the College of Arts and Sciences, the Division of Research and Sponsored Programs, the University Libraries, and the Research Council of Kent State University. The sabbaticals and research funds allowed me to visit several archival depositories. I am thankful to Diane May of the Interlibrary Loan office at Kent State, who was instrumental to the success of this work because of her ability to track down sources. I extend a note of thanks to the National Office of Phi Alpha Theta for awarding me a Phi Alpha Theta Faculty Advisor Research Grant to conduct research for the book. I am also grateful to the Franklin Research Center of Duke University for awarding me a travel grant. I must acknowledge the assistance of the staff at the following libraries of the Cuyahoga County Public Library System, where I spent numerous hours working on this book: North Olmsted, Fairview Park, Berea, and Olmsted Falls branches. Recognition of Baldwin Wallace University, Berea, Ohio, is in order. I spent many days pouring over notes and sources at the university's Ritter Library. My special table was on the first floor, the place where the history books are housed.

I am profoundly grateful to Martha Hodes and Stanley Harrold, who read the manuscript and offered inestimable suggestions for improving it. This book is significantly better because of their careful and thoughtful review. Their insightful observations added a measure of clarity to the study and kept me focused on the task at hand. I would like to extend a thank-you to John Barr for sharing some of his work on Lincoln with me.

I owe a huge debt of gratitude to the many librarians and archivists I met along this journey. Without exception they were helpful, knowledgeable, and professional. They did not hesitate to provide me with collections that I did not know about. Their assistance was immeasurable. I would like to thank the professional staff at Southern Illinois University Press, especially the project editor Khara Lukancic and the copyeditor Mandi Jourdan, for their commitment to making certain that this book is representative of the quality of monographs published by the press. I particularly wish to express a word of thanks to Sylvia Frank Rodrigue, executive editor at the press. She kept me on track and helped me to avoid pitfalls. Her expert advice and encouragement, along with her kind attention to detail and timely responses, were most appreciated and valued.

This acknowledgments section would be incomplete without recognizing my wife, Cassandra, and our son, Evan. My most consistent and resolute supporter was my wife, who read my early work with a discerning eye. Throughout the process, she provided a strong shoulder to lean on at times when I became exhausted and discouraged. As we neared the finish line, her excellent technological skills ensured the timely completion in the final stages and saved me from countless hours of frustration. I am forever grateful for her patience, generous spirit, and confidence in me to persevere to the end. Evan accompanied us on several research trips. Although he was a teenager at the time, he endured long hours of riding in the car and waiting for me to visit archives and libraries without complaint. I thank him for his patience, understanding, and encouragement.

The culmination of this book brings a tremendous amount of joy to the rest of the Hudson and August families. Though there are too many family members and friends to identify by name, rest assured that your support and well wishes were appreciated throughout this endeavor. It is my hope that the individuals and institutions mentioned here are as proud of this work as I am. Any errors of fact or interpretation are solely my responsibility.

BLACK AMERICANS IN MOURNING

Introduction

AN ILLUSTRATION OF THE emotional outpouring of Blacks for Abraham Lincoln can be found in the historical record of Mattie J. Jackson, which includes her reaction to his assassination. Jackson, who was born in bondage in Saint Louis in the 1840s, gained her freedom during the Civil War by escaping via the Underground Railroad. The Indianapolis resident conveyed the sentiments of innumerable Black Americans when she rhapsodized, "The death of the President was like an electric shock to my soul. I could not feel convinced of his death until I gazed upon his remains and heard the last roll of the muffled drum and the farewell boom of the cannon. I was convinced that though we were left to the tender mercies of God, we were without a leader."[1] Most assuredly, African Americans had accepted Lincoln as their president.

As the hostilities of the Civil War came to an end, John Wilkes Booth's outrage over the war's resolution led him to hatch a plot with his conspirators to assassinate Lincoln and other high-ranking officials of his administration. He accomplished his part of the scheme with astonishing precision. At ten thirty on the night of April 14, 1865, Booth carried out the first presidential assassination in the nation's history. The euphoria resulting from Union victories and the surrender of General Robert E. Lee evaporated with news of Lincoln's murder. What started out as a night of entertainment for the Lincolns turned into a night of unbelievable horror. Nine hours after being shot in Ford's Theatre, Lincoln joined the hundreds of thousands of soldiers who had gone before him in death.

The influential Black newspaper the *Christian Recorder* informed its readers that "the nation mourns the loss of her Chief Magistrate, and the hope of our people is again stricken down. Many and heartfelt were the exclamations of sorrow uttered by our people at the loss of so good and great a man."[2] On many occasions, Black mourners' reactions referenced the fact that Lincoln's death was a private as well as a national loss. By combining individual and national grief, the responders embraced a sense of patriotism.

In general, Lincoln's mourners adhered to the nineteenth-century conventions of bereavement. They embraced the customs of draping their homes with black cloth, gathering in places of worship, and talking about the assassination with others. By engaging in these activities, they were better able to shoulder the awful event.[3] There was also another important aspect to Americans following the rituals of bereavement. By doing so, they were "building momentum" for the ceremonies that would take place across the country, the national funeral for the president in Washington, and the processions along the train route to Springfield.[4] Americans with limited financial resources observed stripped-down mourning traditions. This, however, did not mean that poor people were less affected by the crime. Certainly, this was not the case for people of color. For them, in both the "North and South alike," the death of Lincoln was "shattering."[5] The most common emblems of mourning were the tears of men, women, and children. Weeping was one form of grieving that required no expense.

From coast to coast in cities, towns, villages, and hamlets, Americans mourned the passing of the "Sage of Springfield." According to one scholar, "The immediate reaction to Lincoln's death among northerners and African Americans everywhere was grief, pure and simple."[6] People of color in Washington did not have a monopoly on mourning because of their proximity to the scene of the crime. Washington, however, was the epicenter of mourning for people of African descent. The District of Columbia was the only place where two public viewings occurred. Blacks there also had adopted Lincoln as their neighbor. For them, the death of a beloved member of the community was stunning. As word of the assassination coursed through the country to Blacks in faraway places, their grief was not diminished by distance. Reverend Stephen W. Rogers, editor of the *Black Republican*, an African American newspaper in New Orleans, offered a tribute in memory of the deceased president, telling his readers that Lincoln "has fallen by the same spirit that has so long oppressed and destroyed us." He concluded that "the great and glorious" man had "paid the penalty of Apostleship."[7] The Black devotees of Lincoln showered him with adulation. Yet he did not personally know more than a handful of African Americans during his life. For many years after the war, it was not unusual for Black Americans to show their admiration for Lincoln by displaying a photograph of him in their homes.

Lincoln welcomed African Americans to his home on Pennsylvania Avenue against the backdrop of the separation of the races. It was the president who presided over the integration of the White House beginning in the spring of 1862. From then to the end of his presidency, Lincoln treated Black men and women who visited him on an equal basis with whites. Lincoln's interaction with people of color in the presidential office was an important milestone in the history of race relations in the nation. Many whites, including the Democratic press, found it appalling that he would invite Black people to the Executive Mansion.

Blacks identified with Lincoln because of his honesty and lack of pretention. In Lincoln they saw a man "who rose to become one of the world's greatest leaders and yet who never lost his down-to-earth approach to life, nor his interest in the lives of ordinary Americans."[8] The single most important reason why African Americans identified with the sixteenth president, however, had to do with his role in their freedom. Lincoln on many occasions let it be known that he was against slavery. In August 1863, he sent a long letter to his friend James C. Conkling in Springfield, defending his controversial emancipation policy and the use of Black troops in the U.S. Army. Many of Lincoln's fellow Americans believed that he had exceeded his presidential authority with the document of freedom. Although the letter was addressed to Conkling, it was written for him to read at a pro-Union rally on September 3, 1863. The letter

Civil War veteran James Brown of Illinois at age 104 showing his
admiration for Abraham Lincoln. Collection of the Smithsonian National
Museum of African American History and Culture,
Gift from the Liljenquist Family Collection.

also gave the president an opportunity to appeal to anti-Black Northerners. The president told Conkling that he "certainly wish[ed] that all men could be free."[9]

There was no disputing the fact that the president's death "transfixed Negroes with sorrow" and "burdened every black with a personal sense of loss."[10] An examination of the voluminous expressions of condolence from African Americans reveals that they routinely used the adjectives "great and good" when memorializing Lincoln. They could point to several gains made during Lincoln's presidency regarding their race. These included emancipation, the enlistment of Black men into the Union army, diplomatic recognition of two Black countries, and congressional approval of the Thirteenth Amendment. The ratification of the amendment in December 1865 guaranteed that emancipation would not be overturned by future presidents. These advancements did much to cement Lincoln's exalted reputation in the minds of African Americans for years to come. Frederick Douglass, however, was not totally satisfied with the historic ratification. He maintained that if Black men did not possess the same rights as white men, "slavery [was] not abolished."[11]

A tangible response to the assassination of Lincoln was the convening of state and national organizations dedicated to advocating for political, social, and economic justice on behalf of citizens of color. While some Northern states had granted Black men the right to vote, many had not. Black leaders argued that it was necessary to give suffrage to African Africans in order to prevent the old Southern elites from returning to power. Black conventions served several purposes. Among them were registering opposition to racial inequality, invoking Lincoln's name to spur the federal government and state legislatures into action, and acknowledging the president's role in emancipation. After the war, the assemblies also made a point of highlighting the contributions of the United States Colored Troops (USCT) to the war effort. The military service of Black men was a source of pride in the African American community.

The overwhelming number of responses examined in this book were expressed by America's citizens of color in the hours, days, weeks, and months following the tragedy. The notable exception to this is the use of Civil War regimental histories and speeches by members of the Military Order of the Loyal Legion of the United States. In several cases, these sources were published at the turn of the century. This book also benefits from the work of the Federal Writers' Project of the 1930s, which produced *The American Slave: A Composite Autobiography*, commonly known as the Slave Narratives. Historians' arguments against using these controversial sources have been carefully documented over the years. The sources' primary shortcomings are that they may not always be accurate because of the advanced age of some of the formerly enslaved people at the time the interviews were conducted and that the overwhelming number of interviewers were white. Yet the Slave Narratives are important to this study for their personal and individual reflections. In them, many of those who were in bondage recalled how they felt upon learning that Lincoln had been cut down by an assassin. The Slave Narratives provide a window into the cultural life of African Americans who had languished in captivity. Under the direction of the Works Progress Administration, the Federal Writers' Project conducted interviews with nearly two thousand ex-bondmen during the Great Depression. These oral histories are a valuable record of those who survived the infernal institution.

The bicentennial of Lincoln's birth in 2009 and the sesquicentennial of his assassination in 2015 saw a surge in the publication of works about the sixteenth president. Many of the publications during these historical milestones focused on Lincoln's "thoughts on race and slavery."[12] My study places emphasis primarily on the thoughts of African Americans about Lincoln after the assassination. This is the first book devoted to the reactions of Black Americans to the death of Lincoln. This volume amplifies the voices of African American mourners who frequently combined grief over the president's death with gratitude for their freedom.[13]

Although this work is the first full-length treatment of the subject, over the years many works have touched on the reactions of

Black people to Lincoln's death. One of the first publications consisting of testimonies by, and interviews of, African Americans of that era is *They Knew Lincoln*, authored by the Black teacher and dentist John E. Washington in 1942. Washington's volume succeeds in giving a "voice to those who perceived themselves as most powerfully impacted by the dead president."[14] Twenty years later, Benjamin Quarles devoted the last chapter in his book *Lincoln and the Negro* to a discussion of the response of citizens of color to the murder. He insisted that "it was a totally sunless day when Abraham Lincoln's hour struck."[15] John David Smith's *Lincoln and the U.S. Colored Troops* (2013) follows the president on his quest to recruit and train African American men. In the afterword to his study, Smith looks at the effect of the assassination on Black soldiers. The soldiers of the USCT remembered that Lincoln had given them the chance to fight for the preservation of the Union, the liberation of the enslaved, and the opportunity to become men. "No group of soldiers lamented Lincoln's death," claimed Steven F. Ramold, "more than the African Americans of the United States Colored Troops."[16] Richard Wightman Fox acknowledges in his book *Lincoln's Body* (2015) that the Illinois native was a "symbol of republican simplicity" and that for more than a hundred years, "African Americans did the most to preserve a continuous memory of Lincoln the emancipator." He also states that Black people "turned out in large numbers" to view the body because they wanted to personally bid farewell to the president.[17]

Martha Hodes's volume *Mourning Lincoln* (2015) brings to life the reactions of African Americans to the death and funeral of the president more than any other monograph. Her study chronicles a diverse range of clashing reactions to Lincoln's demise. Hodes provides compelling insights into the various reactions to the assassination, which allows readers to gain an understanding of why so many people were affected by it. Jonathan W. White has collected more than 120 letters that were sent to Lincoln from enslaved people and free African Americans during the war in his edited volume *To Address You as My Friend* (2021). The letter writers were certain that they had an advocate in the White House who understood them and their plight. White plainly states in the epilogue that people of color reacted to Lincoln's death as if they had lost a friend. *Spectacle of Grief* (2022), by Sarah Purcell, is an examination of nine public funerals of notable figures of the Civil War generation. The author uses the obsequies of these individuals to show how "competing memories" affected mourning rituals and national identities during the nineteenth century and beyond.[18] The death of Lincoln and reactions to it receive little attention in Purcell's volume. According to White in his book *A House Built by Slaves* (2022), Lincoln invited African American men and women to the Presidential Mansion not for show but rather for him and his Black visitors to engage in meaningful conversations about race, citizenship rights, political and miliary matters, and other issues. In the chapter on the response of African Americans to the assassination, White maintains that they were burdened with sorrow.

Black Americans in Mourning argues that there was unity among Black grievers and that individuals and groups ceased disparaging Lincoln in the immediate aftermath of his death. Lincoln's place in historical memory has been the focal point of many works; there is no need to duplicate what has been thoroughly covered by other historians. Although my study includes some historical memory of Lincoln, it was my intention not to make it the centerpiece of this book.

Based on the evidence, a thematic approach with respect to chronology seemed to be the best way of organizing this monograph. Some of the themes covered here are the funeral train and perceptions of Lincoln as an earthly Moses, as the Great Emancipator, as a father-image and friend, and as a symbol of the national government. Archival sources and recent secondary literature about Lincoln are the foundation of this book. With varying levels of articulation, African Americans shared with the nation their hurt, sadness, and reverence for the martyred leader. The reactions of the most prominent Black Americans, who were also the most articulate, can be found in this book. Of all the African American eulogists, none surpassed Frederick Douglass in erudition. The renowned abolitionist, orator, and writer had not vacillated when he believed that it was necessary to criticize the president. But after the assassination, Douglass offered heartfelt declarations of condolence for his slain friend. In the estimation of one historian, the death of Lincoln "silenced his black critics and threw a stunned black community into deep mourning" for several days.[19] My book tells the story of a race in mourning through an analysis of individual recollections and the formal expressions of institutions and organizations.

It was apparent that formal acknowledgments of Lincoln's death were not reserved for organizations controlled by men only. African American women did not remain taciturn as events unfolded in Washington. The Ladies' Union Association of Philadelphia was formed by African American women to aid sick and wounded Black soldiers in 1864. This organization offered one of the first expressions of lament for the president by issuing a set of official statements regarding the tragedy. The women called attention to Lincoln's leadership skills as the Civil War president. "We deeply deplore the loss of him who has with wonderful ability," the Committee on Resolutions wrote, "brought us safely thus far through a season of peril such as the country has never before experienced." They also claimed that Lincoln "should stand first in the hearts of his countrymen through all time."[20] The women of the association had placed Lincoln's death in a context beyond the personalized level by also memorializing him as a significant national leader.

Letters, diaries, journals, autobiographies, reminiscences, and speeches provide a wealth of information about the reactions of Black citizens. Because this book allows men and women of color to speak for themselves, readers will understand the sorrow that gripped them following the assassination. The original form in which African Americans expressed their heartache has been maintained, though phrases and words that were underlined in the original source have been italicized. The grammatical infelicities of Black and white Americans, particularly those who had been held as chattel, have been preserved. Many of the primary sources from this era of U.S. history include the N-word. The term was used frequently by both Black and white Americans in the nineteenth century, and I came across it hundreds of times in my research. I have inserted "N-word" in brackets to show where the odious term appears in the original quotation.

During the Civil War, Lincoln formed a special bond with African Americans and white Northerners. In return they admired and respected the president for his handling of the national crisis.[21] Like people of color, numerous Northern whites were also effusive in expressing their lament for the president. The reactions of African Americans and whites were similar in many respects. Both groups of mourners frequently used the term "gloom" as a way of expressing their sorrow and that of others brought on by the shattering event. The term suggested a somber and dark cloud, which remained among mourners after the initial shock of the assassination had waned.[22] The wounding of the secretary of state, William H. Seward, and his son Frederick by Lewis Powell was not lost on the responders, who often conveyed sympathy for them. In reacting to the assassination, Black and white mourners did not hesitate to denounce John Wilkes Booth as a villain and scoundrel. The *Weekly Anglo-African* referred to Booth as "the devil-possessed assassin."[23] Another Black journal reported that Lincoln had fallen "by the hand of a bloody" slayer.[24] The number of reflections of white Americans far exceeded those of Black mourners. The numerical superiority of the white population helps to explain the difference in responses. Furthermore, the voices of white grievers could be found in places where African Americans were invisible: federal and state governments, military institutions, and the judicial system, to mention a few.

The response of African Americans was distinctive in a few significant ways. They frequently mentioned slavery and freedom when expressing their reactions. With Lincoln gone, some members of the emancipated race found themselves in liberation limbo. White Americans, of course, were not burdened with a fear of being sent back to the plantation. The indignity of being stripped of their humanity was unknown to white citizens. From a personal standpoint, whites could not write or speak about being delivered from bondage and the victimization of racism.

Another difference was that the reactions of some Blacks to the death of Lincoln flowed through the pens of white Americans. Their observations occupy an important part of the historical record of mourning in the African American community. It was not uncommon for white Americans who interacted frequently with Black people to document their reactions.[25] The dominant race viewed the former captives as socially and intellectually inferior to them. White recorders commonly portrayed people of color as totally grief-stricken, as devoted Christians, or as resolute and manly.[26] The profusion of sorrow demonstrated by African Americans was not universally replicated by white people. While some white Southerners lamented the death, many others approved of the murder. This is not to suggest that Northerners always refrained from expressing satisfaction with the assassination. There were numerous examples of civilians and some Union soldiers who welcomed Lincoln's death. It should not be overlooked that some members of the radical faction of the Republican Party were not sad to see Lincoln go.

White abolitionists, teachers, editors, reformers, and Southern aristocrats did their part to preserve for posterity the reflections of Black people. Their letters, diaries, journals, official documents, sermons, and newspaper articles captured the sorrow of the emancipated race. White teachers recalled the agony of their Black students when they learned of the dreadful news. Clearly, mourning was not reserved for adults only. White officers of the USCT told the story of how the soldiers reacted upon receiving word that their commander in chief had been murdered. White federal agents and missionaries who worked with Blacks in refugee camps also had an opportunity to record their responses. The Massachusetts native Horace James shed light on the conundrum of African Americans in the wake of Lincoln's death. The end of the war found him in North Carolina working on behalf of the freedpeople as a superintendent of Negro affairs. His observation of the freedpeople there led him to conclude that they existed in a "transition state, scarcely knowing whether they were or were not free—a point made still more uncertain to them by the untimely death of their great Deliverer, Abraham Lincoln."[27]

Although Black people did not speak with a monolithic voice on political, social, or cultural matters, Lincoln's death was an exception. The research for this book did not uncover any Black person who was grateful that Lincoln had been slain. This was a remarkable revelation, especially when it is remembered that Lincoln had his share of critics among both races during the antebellum period and his tenure in the White House. When his three-week-long funeral was over, African Americans turned their attention to a future without their president. They had no choice but to prepare to meet the difficult challenges that were certain to come their way.

During the 1850s Lincoln's prejudicial view of African Americans led him to publicly announce that they should not have the franchise or serve in public office or as jurors. Informed people of color remembered Lincoln's comment about race during his fourth senatorial debate with Stephen A. Douglas in Charleston, Illinois, in September 1858. There in eastern Illinois, Lincoln believed that it was necessary to respond to the incumbent senator who had accused him of promoting social and political equality among the races. In reference to Black people, the challenger said that "inasmuch as they cannot so live, while they do remain together there must be the position of superior and inferior, and I as much as any other man am in favor of having the superior position assigned to the white race."[28] Lincoln's attitude was not an anomaly. The acceptance of Black inferiority was the position of most Americans.

Douglas's reelection to the U.S. Senate was only a temporary setback for Lincoln. As it turned out, he would claim the greater prize two years later. His decision to seek the nomination of the Republican Party in the presidential election of 1860 was a seminal moment in American political history. Black Americans closely followed the campaign. They knew that issues of slavery and the possibility of secession dominated the conversation in political circles. Although voting was extremely limited for people of color, they overwhelmingly supported the Republican Party. They believed that a Lincoln victory would bring freedom to those in bondage. On a Missouri plantation, an enslaved person was physically abused by his owner for displaying a photograph of Lincoln in his home.[29] As the Republican National Convention prepared to meet in Chicago, Black opposition to Lincoln continued to bubble up. John Mercer Langston, the future dean of the law school at Howard University, could not hide his disillusionment with Lincoln. His preference to lead the ticket was Salmon P. Chase or William H. Seward. The Ohio native believed that Lincoln did not possess the requisite credentials to lead the Republican ticket because of his cautious attitude "toward the oppressed."[30] Another one of Lincoln's critics was Hezekiah Ford Douglas of Illinois, an accomplished orator and a fiery abolitionist who later served in the Union army. The African American leader remembered that Lincoln had refused to endorse a petition calling for the repeal of the prohibition on Blacks testifying in cases that involved white citizens of Illinois. Douglas's rant against Lincoln was on display during the presidential election of 1860. He asserted that the Republican nominee was "a supporter of white supremacy and an opponent of equality for blacks."[31] Douglas accused Lincoln of representing the "Slave Power" of the South.[32] This speech by Douglas was reprinted in the *Liberator*, which spoke to his influence during the campaign. The *Weekly Anglo-African* also weighed in on the 1860 presidential contest. According to its editor, the difference between the two major political parties was miniscule at best. The newspaper argued that both parties "entertained the same ideas" and that the Republicans' stand against the spread of slavery amounted to no more than "opposition to the black man."[33]

As the presidential campaign of 1860 moved toward Election Day, Frederick Douglass claimed that the Republican Party was indistinguishable from the Democratic Party and that the Republicans had no intention of eliminating slavery. Some African Americans were dissatisfied with Lincoln's candidacy for president because they viewed him as "insufficiently radical on the slavery question."[34] A few days before the nation voted, H. Ford Douglas told an audience in Boston that the Republican Party, although not ideal, was the preferred choice in the four-man contest. In what amounted to a lukewarm endorsement of the Illinoisan, Douglas told the crowd, "I love everything the South hates, and since they have evidenced their dislike of Mr. Lincoln, I am bound to love you Republicans with all your faults."[35] In other words, Douglas believed that Lincoln was the lesser of the four evils.

Following Lincoln's election in November, the Black newspaper correspondent George E. Stephens of Philadelphia, who reached the rank of first lieutenant in the Fifty-Fourth Massachusetts Regiment, offered a harsh indictment of the government. He claimed that Lincoln's 1860 election victory represented "the fag end of a series of pro-slavery administrations."[36] With the election over, Black Americans eagerly waited to hear what Lincoln would say to a divided nation in his inaugural speech. The answer came four months later on March 4, 1861. Lincoln's conciliatory message on slavery left people of color in a state of frustration. He made it plain that he hoped to reunite the country by reassuring Southerners that there was no cause for "apprehension" regarding his meddling with slavery. The president claimed that he had no intention of interfering "with the institution of slavery in the States where it exists."[37] Douglass could not hide his disappointment when he claimed that the inaugural address was "vastly below what we had fondly hoped it might be. It is a double-tongued document, capable of two constructions, and conceals rather than declares a definite policy."[38] Lincoln's reticent approach to dealing with slavery dimmed the optimism of African Americans that the institution might one day disappear.

African American leaders and ordinary citizens were put off by Lincoln's position of compromise toward the dehumanizing institution. The president believed that compensation to the slaveowners should be a part of emancipation. Not long after the start of the war, Jabez P. Campbell, a leading minister of the African Methodist Episcopal Church in New Jersey, articulated the opinion of many in the African American community regarding the federal government's noncommitment toward the elimination of the scourge. He accused the Lincoln administration of waging "a war for the Union, to save slavery for the Union."[39] In a Fourth of July speech at Himrod's Corner, New York, in 1862, Frederick Douglass did not hold back his displeasure with Lincoln's conservative approach to freeing those in captivity. He told the crowd that the president's policy on slavery was designed to "shield and protect" the institution from destruction.[40] In a speech in July 1862, on the Oberlin College campus in Ohio, John Mercer Langston thundered against the president for his lack of enthusiasm for emancipation. He also called on the chief executive to acknowledge "the humanity of the slaves, using the latent strength of the colored people north and south."[41]

Some African American leaders rejected Lincoln's suggestion that the presence of Black people in the country was the cause of the Civil War. George B. Vashon, an abolitionist and the first Black graduate of Oberlin College, claimed that the answer as to who caused the conflict "must be sought in the wrongs" inflicted on people of color "by the white man."[42] Douglass was also insulted by Lincoln's assertion that his race was responsible for the war. He fumed that Lincoln was "a genuine representative of American prejudice and Negro hatred."[43]

Decades after Appomattox, some African Americans expressed their disenchantment with Lincoln in interviews with government workers. The former bondman Morris Shephard of Fort Gibson, Oklahoma, remembered the months after the Civil War as a time of uncertainty for the emancipated people. When mentioning Lincoln to an interviewer from the Federal Writers' Project, the Oklahoman related his dashed hopes. Shephard intoned, "I always think of my old master as de one dat freed me, and anyways Abraham Lincoln and none of his North people didn't look after me and buy my crop right after I was free like old Master did. Dat was the time dat was de hardest and everything was dark and confusion."[44] When an interviewer asked Ed Barber of South Carolina for his opinion of the president, he replied with an acerbic comment: "What I think of Abe Lincoln? I think he was a poor buckra white man, to de likes of me. Although, I 'spects Mr. Lincoln meant well but I can't help but wish him had continued splittin' fence rails, which they said he knowed all 'bout, and never took a hand in runnin' de government of which he knowed nothing bout."[45] It was quite possible that Shephard and Barber were echoing criticisms about Lincoln that they had heard from white Southerners. During the years of the Lost Cause, Lincoln became the villain and the Confederacy the victim.[46]

Black people did not speak with a single voice regarding Lincoln's role in the emancipation moment. Hannah McFarland, who was born in Georgetown, South Carolina, and later relocated to Oklahoma City, was ambivalent at best about the man from Illinois. She intimated to an interviewer, "Slavery sho' didn't he'p us none to my belief, I didn't care much 'bout Lincoln. It was nice of him to free us, but 'course he didn't want to."[47] The former bondman Thomas Hall of North Carolina offered a sharp reproach of the dead president. His anger had not subsided with old age. The elderly Hall inveighed that "Lincoln got the praise for freeing us, but did he do it? He give us freedom without giving us any chance to live ourselves and we still had to depend on the southern white man for work, food, and clothing, and he held us through our necessity and want in a state of servitude but little better than slavery." Hall concluded his statement with an indictment of Northerners, telling the interlocutor that they had a hand in putting Black people "back in slavery again."[48] Hall was letting it be known that emancipation without human rights was unacceptable.

There was no shortage of disapproval of Lincoln's colonization scheme from members of the Black community. Colonization was one of the most controversial policies of his presidency. Lincoln was wise enough to know that it was not a realistic solution to the race dilemma in the United States. It would have been impossible to relocate hundreds of thousands of people to distant places, even with the assistance of the American Colonization Society.[49] Yet the president continued to endorse the idea. People of color found the Civil War president's repatriation views disparaging. Isaiah C. Wears, an influential Black Philadelphian, averred, "To be asked, after so many years of oppression and wrong," to leave the nation was without merit.[50] The Black resident of Philadelphia and abolitionist Frances E. Watkins Harper derided Lincoln for his plan. Writing to the *Christian Recorder* in 1862, she told the president that people of African descent did not "see the wisdom nor expediency of our self-exportation from a land which has been in a measure enriched by our toil for generations." She also reminded Lincoln that Black people were still waiting for "justice and equity which has been withheld from us for ages."[51]

Despite overt racism, African Americans were not about to let colonization advocates force them from the country of their birth. The Black people of Lincoln's hometown, in dismissing colonization, made it clear that they intended "to die and to be buried" in Springfield.[52] In 1862, the Black abolitionist Robert Purvis sent a letter to Senator Samuel C. Pomeroy of Kansas expressing his dislike for the design to colonize members of his race. Purvis's repudiation centered on the fact that his people had a right to remain in the country because "their tears, and sweat, and blood" had helped to nourish American growth.[53] In August 1862, a small number of Black men from Philadelphia made their position on colonization known to the president. The group told him that racism had its origin in the "Institution of Slavery." They urged Lincoln to adopt "a more liberal and enlightened public policy" regarding the future of African Americans in the nation.[54]

The Negro Convention Movement was a powerful opponent of colonization before, during, and after the war. The movement had its origin in Philadelphia in September 1830, when its founder, Richard Allen, a bishop of the African Methodist Episcopal Church, presided over the first meeting. From then on, African Americans' opposition to the unpopular doctrine did not lessen with the passage of time. Delegates to both state and national conventions claimed that the American Colonization Society, the predominant colonization organization, was motivated by malice and shortsightedness. The failure of the colonization movement confirmed that Black people in the United States were here to stay. If Lincoln's colonization plan had been successful, the country in the future might have been without the institution of slavery and citizens of color.[55]

Perhaps this possibility was not on the minds of those African Americans who believed that colonization was a sensible proposition. The Black American John D. Johnson, commissioner from Liberia, wrote to Lincoln in March 1863, telling him that "numbers" of African Americans were ready to relocate to Liberia. He concluded his letter by advising that both Black Americans and the West African country would benefit from colonization. "The people need homs," he told the president, "Liberia needs emigrants."[56] Seven months later in October 1863, B. F. Brown of New Jersey also sent a letter to Lincoln requesting help to expatriate Blacks to Africa. Brown made it clear that financial assistance from the federal government was needed to facilitate their relocation.[57] He told the nation's chief that some Black people of his state were preparing to leave the country. Brown did not elaborate on the nature of the preparations.

By the time of Lincoln's death, he had admitted to himself that Black citizens were too deeply entrenched in American life to be uprooted. Doubtless, Lincoln had made giant strides on the question of race since leaving the Illinois prairie. As Orville Vernon Burton puts it in his book *The Age of Lincoln*, the evidence is overwhelming that the president's "views had evolved and expanded" during his time in the Executive Mansion regarding "the place of African Americans in a nation undergoing a new birth of freedom."[58]

During the president's time in the White House, he attracted both followers and detractors. Counted among his critics were several Republicans, abolitionists, Northerners, Democrats, editors, Blacks, and white Southerners. In 1864, the *New Orleans Tribune*, an African American journal and sharp critic of Lincoln's administration, denounced the nation's political leaders. The editor told those in power in Washington that the subordinate status of Black citizens remained a protracted recrimination on the conscience of America. "Freedom without equality," the editorial insisted, "before the law and at the ballot box is impossible."[59]

Lincoln's disapproval among some of his fellow Republicans led them to entertain the notion of removing him as the standard-bearer of their party in the presidential election of 1864.[60] A number of Black leaders were also disillusioned with Lincoln during the campaign. Their disappointment found expression in a meeting in Cleveland, Ohio, in 1864. There, a few hundred men selected John C. Frémont, the first presidential nominee of the Republican Party in 1856, as their presidential choice.

Some African American leaders refrained from criticizing Lincoln in the run-up to the 1864 presidential election. By then, Lincoln's name had become common in many Black households. And Lincoln himself could point to several accomplishments that directly affected Black people. In October 1864, the voters of Maryland approved a new constitution, which included a provision abolishing slavery in the state. To celebrate the end of bondage in Maryland, a large group of Black men and women gathered on November 1 at the Fifteenth Street Presbyterian Church in the nation's capital. Henry Highland Garnet, an abolitionist, minister, and educator, presided over the meeting. The prominent Black leader was obviously aware of the criticism that Lincoln was subjected to from people of color. Against that backdrop, Reverend Garnet called on his fellow Black Americans "to stop finding fault with the President, for there was not a man living who could do better than the man in the executive chair."[61] As a way of showing their gratitude to Lincoln as the apostle of emancipation, the throng left the church and reassembled at the White House, where they serenaded the president with singing and cheering. When the votes in the presidential election had been tallied, it became clear that Lincoln's opponents were unable to derail him. He won reelection by defeating George B. McClellan.

Black people were hopeful that the second term of Lincoln's presidency would lead to an improvement in their political and social standing. Shortly after the election, the *New Orleans Tribune* published an editorial titled "The Era and the Right of Suffrage," which advocated for Black voting privileges. "We claim the electoral franchise as an act of justice, as an application of a general principle," the newspaper said, "we do not claim it for a few individuals, but for all."[62] During Lincoln's years in office, slavery and citizenship rights for people of color were two of the most profound issues confronting him. The conflict, with all its bloodshed and carnage, had set the stage for Black people to embrace the concepts of freedom and equality. The relationship between African Americans and Lincoln was a complicated symbiosis during the middle of the nineteenth century.

By the time of Lincoln's second inauguration, the Confederate republic was on its deathbed. Lincoln did not know it, but evil forces would soon prepare for him a deathbed of his own. Six weeks after the start of his second term, his life came to an end. Of all the casualties of that tumultuous time, the death of Abraham Lincoln was the most unforgettable. Innumerable citizens of African heritage mourned for the man whom they regarded as their friend, father, deliverer, protector, and benefactor.

CHAPTER ONE

Pandemonium on the Potomac River

A FEW WEEKS AFTER DELIVERING his second inaugural
address on March 4, 1865, Abraham Lincoln accepted
General Ulysses S. Grant's invitation to visit the Army
of the Potomac headquartered at City Point, Virginia. In search of
rest, the president looked forward to leaving Washington. Upon
his arrival in the port town, it quickly became apparent that the
anticipated relaxation would elude the commander in chief. Recep-
tions, reviews of the troops, and visits with wounded soldiers placed
heavy demands on his time. Nonetheless, his visit there recharged
him.[1] Thomas Morris Chester recorded that the men of the Twenty-
Fourth and Twenty-Fifth Corps at City Point were "a grand sight"
and their soldierly deportment was "a source of considerable satisfaction" to the president.[2] Chester had a close-up view of the Civil War
as a correspondent for the *Philadelphia Press*. He covered some of
the most memorable events of our nation's epic moment as the war
ended. The thrill Lincoln got from mingling with the soldiers and
their admiration of him lifted his spirit. The Blacks at City Point
could barely contain their excitement upon seeing their
president.

The end of the war found George A. Huron of Indiana serving
as a sanitary agent for the Union armies at City Point. Huron could
not help but notice the esteem that African Americans had for the
president. Huron remembered them cutting photographs of Lincoln from newspapers and placing them "upon the walls of their
huts and tents, and [they] were carried as treasured momentoes
upon the persons of those who had proven in their own lives—the

This portrait of a careworn Abraham Lincoln (1809–65) was taken by Alexander Gardner in February 1865. Lincoln's death two months later plunged the country into profound sorrow, particularly among African Americans. LC-DIG-ppmsca-19215, Prints and Photographs Division, Library of Congress.

contrast in the meaning of the words freedom and slavery." Huron remembered an elderly Black woman from Louisiana "with head white as driven snow" who cried out in jubilation upon touching President Lincoln. With a biblical reference, she proclaimed, "I'se free! I'se free! I'se free!! And I'se ready to die, foh I'se tetched de hem of his gahment."[3] For a moment, the transfixed woman substituted Abraham Lincoln for Jesus Christ.

As the calendar turned from March to April, the Confederate government was on the brink of collapse and General Robert E. Lee was standing at the threshold of defeat. The impending vanquishment precipitated the abandonment of Richmond by President Jefferson Davis on April 2, 1865. The next day, General August V. Kautz of Ohio, who was originally from Germany, led a division of the United States Colored Troops (USCT) of the Twenty-Fifth Corps of the Army of the James into the beleaguered Confederate capital. He found the fallen city in ruins. The general told a friend in Philadelphia, "I marched in at the head of my Division," which consisted of the USCT, who were "among the first to enter" Richmond.[4] Kautz later served on the military commission that found the conspirators guilty of assassinating the president. The white chaplain Sam S. Gardian of the Seventy-Third USCT told the adjutant general after the fall of Richmond that the troops of the regiment "exhibited a manly and patient spirit which could not be excelled."[5] Chaplain Garland H. White of the Twenty-Eighth United States Colored Infantry confessed that his heart overflowed with "joy" when "the doors of all the slave pens were thrown open" in the city of Richmond.[6] Even before Lincoln's arrival in Richmond, there and elsewhere Black people were acknowledging him as "a liberating god."[7]

The demise of the Confederate government did not escape the attention of the delegates attending the annual conference of the African Methodist Episcopal Church then meeting in Baltimore. On April 13, the conference announced that God had crowned "the Federal army with triumphant success in the capture of Richmond" and "with the complete routing and demoralization of its greatest generals and army."[8] To the Black clerics, the Almighty was on the side of the Union.

The commander in chief's visit to Richmond on April 4 made a lasting impression on Alexander H. Newton. He was born free in North Carolina in the 1830s and enlisted in the Twenty-Ninth Regiment of the Connecticut Volunteers (Colored) in December 1863. To him, this scene was reminiscent of Jesus's triumphal entry into Jerusalem a week before his crucifixion. Newton remembered the presidential visit as one in which Lincoln's admirers displayed an exuberance worthy of the occasion. In recording the event for posterity, Newton wrote, "There were multitudes of Colored people to greet him on every hand. They received him with many demonstrations that came from the heart, thanking God that they had seen the day of their salvation." Newton stated that Lincoln made a short speech at the Confederate capitol in which he told the Black population, "God has made you free and if those who are your superiors are not able to recognize that you are free, we will have to take the sword and musket and again teach them that you are free."[9] Upon seeing Lincoln in Richmond, a woman of color cried out, "I thank you, dear Jesus, that I behold President Linkup."[10] As the president prepared to leave the wharf for his return trip to Washington, an old Black woman yelled, "Don't drown Massa Abe, for God's sake."[11] If that adorer only had the benefit of foresight, she no doubt would have advised the president ten days later, "for God's sake," do not go to Ford's Theatre.

With the walls of defense caving in all around, General Lee had no desire to sacrifice any more of his men in a futile effort to stave off the inevitable. By then, the sun was setting on the Confederacy's struggle for independence. Lee could not find any hope for victory among the remnants of his once-mighty Army of Northern Virginia. The venerable military leader decided to meet with Ulysses S. Grant, general chief of the Union armies, at Appomattox Court House. When Lee arrived, his appearance revealed that he was a beaten man. The stress of war had aged the battle-tested general. On Sunday afternoon, April 9, 1865, Grant sent a telegram to Secretary of War Edwin M. Stanton announcing the surrender of

Lee and his Army of Northern Virginia. Michael Shiner, a former enslaved person, was working at the Navy Yard in Washington when the war came to an end. He recollected Lee's capitulation as a time in which the president, whom he referred to as "the Hon. Abraham Lincoln," displayed a magnanimous spirit toward his adversaries. He confided to his diary that it was Lincoln's request "to general grant to allow all the Confederate officers to keep all there horses and Side arms."[12] Lincoln knew before going to bed on Palm Sunday that the war was over. On April 10, the headline of the *Albany Evening Journal* announced, "General Lee and His Army Have Surrendered! Slavery and Treason Buried in the Same Grave!"[13] The reformer, abolitionist, and journalist Jane Grey Swisshelm heard that an African American woman in the nation's capital who "was much troubled in her mind" had prophesied that an impending doom was on the horizon. As Washingtonians were celebrating the end of the war, the woman repeatedly said, "They's goin' to do somethin' drefful to you. I's affeared for you all. You's 'joicin', an' they's agwine to do somethin' drefful." The prognosticator concluded that Southern hatred for the Union was real because "you've done gone an tuk their [N-word] from em."[14] She did not say what it would be, but something awful was about to occur.

With the Confederacy in the throes of death, threats from would-be assassins bedeviled the nation's leader. Lincoln's habit of going for walks at night without bodyguards frustrated his advisers. Time and time again, Secretary Stanton and others conveyed to the president that peril lurked all around him. President Lincoln once told a friend, "I do not see what the rebels would gain by either killing or getting possession of me. I am but a single individual, and it would not help their cause, or make the least difference in the progress of the war."[15] Lincoln was determined not to compromise the work of the presidency by worrying about being assassinated. His natural inclination was to see the good in the American citizenry. He was a man of the people, and not even the trappings of the presidential office could change that. Therefore, it was not surprising when a large crowd gathered at the White House on the night of April 11,

1865, and gave the commander in chief an enthusiastic reception when he appeared in a window on the second floor. Many Black people of Washington were among the throng.

A prominent person of color who witnessed the event was Elizabeth Keckley, a White House employee, former enslaved person, seamstress, and confidant of Mary Lincoln. Keckley served as president of the Contraband Relief Association of the District of Columbia. Organized in 1862 by Black women, the association's mission was to provide relief to those of their race who were destitute.[16] During the Civil War, thousands of Blacks had flocked to Washington to seek a better life and whatever protection the city could offer them against racial hatred and violence. Keckley intimated to a friend, "What an easy matter would it be to kill the President, as he stands there! He could be shot down from the crowd, and no one be able to tell who fired the shot."[17] When Keckley told Mary about her premonition, the First Lady confessed, "Ah, no one knows what it is to live in constant dread of some fearful tragedy. The President has been warned so often that I tremble for him on every public occasion."[18] President Lincoln wanted to make certain that his formal speech, which included his views on reconstruction and his defense of the government in Louisiana, was not misunderstood by the thousands below and Americans across the country. Reading from his carefully prepared manuscript, he struck a conciliatory tone with his opening lines: "We meet this evening, not in sorrow, but in gladness of heart. The evacuation of Petersburg and Richmond, and the surrender of the principal insurgent army, give hope of a righteous and speedy peace whose joyous expression cannot be restrained."[19] Lincoln was looking forward to the Confederate States rejoining the Union.

Lincoln's speech was marked by a historic moment when he said, "It is also unsatisfactory to some that the elective franchise is not given to the colored man. I would myself prefer that it were now conferred on the very intelligent, and on those who serve our cause as soldiers."[20] Lincoln knew that, without suffrage, Black Southerners had no opportunity of participating in the political life of the country. He hoped to move African Americans closer to the circle of citizenship by advocating for them to have the right to vote, albeit on a limited basis. Lincoln came close to "a complete overturning" of the Supreme Court's infamous *Dred Scott* decision of 1857, which promoted the idea that Black people were not citizens and, further- more, that they could not qualify for full American citizenship in the future.[21] The president's proposal aligned him with the Radical members of his party who had been calling for Blacks to be granted voting privileges. Black suffrage could also open the door for Republicans to gain a foothold in Southern politics. Com- menting on Lincoln's speech, Frederick Douglass said, "It was just like Abraham Lincoln. He never shocked prejudices unnecessarily. Having learned statesmanship while splitting rails, he always used the thin edge of the wedge first."[22] Douglass was telling those who were frustrated with Lincoln, particularly some Radical Republicans, that limited Black suffrage was the beginning, not the end. And that eventually universal manhood suffrage would come to pass.

During the war, Douglass was one of a handful of Black men with whom Lincoln had a personal relationship. Their friendship started to evolve when he visited the president at the White House on August 10, 1863. Their discussion centered on military matters involving men of color. The uninvited guest pressed Lincoln on equal compensation, humane treatment by the Confederacy, and the appointment of Black soldiers as commissioned officers. Lincoln intimated to Douglass that the conditions experienced by African American troops were a "necessary concession" for them to serve and to win the support of white Northerners for the controversial decision to use Black men as soldiers. Douglass later said that Lincoln greeted him at his home "as one gentleman would be received by another."[23] Realizing Douglass's brilliance, the president sought and valued his counsel on racial, social, political, and other matters. In the nation's leader, Douglass found a man who was thoughtful, kind, attentive, and honest.

Lincoln's April 11 speech was historic, not only because it was Lincoln's last but also because it represented the first time that a president announced in public support for voting rights for some African Americans. The public announcement was new, but the

Frederick Douglass (1817 or 1818–95) was a former enslaved person, abolitionist, orator, and writer. Having visited the White House three times, he and Lincoln became good friends. LC-DIG-ppmsca-69250, Prints and Photographs Division, Library of Congress.

idea was old. Lincoln, in a private letter to Union general James S. Wadsworth in January 1864, admitted that Black troops had "heroically vindicated their manhood on the battle-field, where, in assisting to save the life of the Republic, they have demonstrated in blood their right to the ballot."[24] The celebrated Black Presbyterian cleric of New York James W. C. Pennington claimed that Lincoln was the president of Black people "because he is the only American President who has ever given any attention to colored men as citizens."[25] Lincoln gave hope to people of color across the country whose lives had been characterized by misery and disappointment. African Americans wanted to be accepted, respected, and included in the realm of American democracy.

As at Lincoln's second inaugural address, among the listeners the night of his last speech was John Wilkes Booth of Maryland. Although not professionally trained, Booth had honed his skills to become one of the leading actors of the South. While performing in the states below the Mason-Dixon Line, Booth most assuredly heard Southerners spew hatred against the president and the North. Such vitriolic comments doubtless contributed to the Confederate sympathizer's deep dislike for both Lincoln and Northerners.[26] The twenty-six-year-old fumed when he heard the president advance the idea of giving the ballot to Black men who were literate or had a record of service in the U.S. Army. Booth whispered, "That means [N-word] citizenship." He continued, "That is the last speech he will ever make." As Booth left the White House lawn, he turned to David E. Herold, a future accomplice, and snarled, "By God, I'll put him through."[27]

At the start of the conflict, Major Robert Anderson had on April 14, 1861, lowered the Stars and Stripes and evacuated Fort Sumter. Four years later, he made a triumphant return to the scene where he had surrendered. The arrival of the steamer *Arago* from New York City with General Robert Anderson aboard stoked the excitement in anticipation of the flag-raising ceremony. The steamer the *Planter*, piloted by the Black naval captain Robert Smalls, transported several thousand Blacks to the federal fort to witness the activities. Nearly three years earlier, in August 1862, Smalls had

had a meeting with the president at the White House. He used the opportunity to encourage Lincoln to recruit Black men for military service. Among the passengers on Smalls's vessel were Major Martin R. Delany of the 104th USCT, his son Toussaint L'Ouverture Delany of the Fifty-Fourth Massachusetts Regiment, and the elderly Robert Vesey, the son of Denmark Vesey. A carpenter and free man of color, Denmark Vesey had been the leader of an elaborate plot to liberate the captives of Charleston. In July 1822, Vesey, along with more than thirty other insurrectionists, were hanged by the State of South Carolina. The failure of the conspiracy heightened the anxiety of white Southerners over the possibility of slave revolts. The concluding activity of the flag-hoisting celebration was a dinner at the Charleston Hotel where General Anderson offered a tribute to the president. The general's toast contained a bit of irony when he invited the crowd to join him "in drinking [to] the health" of the commander in chief. He concluded with the statement, "I give you the good, the great, the honest man, Abraham Lincoln."[28]

At about the same time that Anderson was making his toast, Booth was entering the presidential box at Ford's Theatre. A cursory historical look at Lincoln reminds us that his life was full of ironies. His presidential career began and ended with flag-raising ceremonies; one in the North in Philadelphia in 1861 and one in the South in Charleston in 1865. While en route to Washington, Lincoln stopped in Philadelphia to raise a new flag at Independence Hall. Against the backdrop of an assassination plot in Baltimore, he gave an address there on February 21, 1861. The president-elect declared that he "would rather be assassinated on this spot than to surrender" the principles of the Declaration of Independence.[29]

Good Friday, April 14, was a joyous day in the life of Christians who were observing its meaning with prayer, meditation, and religious services. Elizabeth Keckley recorded her impression of Lincoln's demeanor that day. "His face was more cheerful than I had seen it for a long while," she wrote, "and he seemed to be in a generous, forgiving mood."[30] At four o'clock he and Mary went for a carriage ride to the Navy Yard. In responding to his wife's comment about his happiness, Lincoln replied, "We must *both*, be more cheer-

Celebration at Fort Sumter in which Black and white spectators witnessed the flag-raising ceremony on April 14, 1865. General Robert Anderson made a triumphant return to the place where he had surrendered four years earlier. LC-DIG-stereo-1s04545, Prints and Photographs Division, Library of Congress.

ful in the future—between the war and the loss of our darling Willie—we have both, been very miserable."[31] Lincoln looked forward to attending the comedic play *Our American Cousin*, starring Laura Keene, at Ford's Theatre that night. The theater was one of Lincoln's favorite entertainment activities.

The owners of Ford's Theatre were thrilled to announce that the president of the United States and General Grant had reservations to attend the play. Newspapers spread the message of the presidential visit to the venue on Tenth Street. Lincoln did not want to disappoint those who were expecting to see him there. Washington was teeming with federal troops who wanted a glimpse of their commander in chief. A public appearance would provide them with the opportunity of seeing their leader.[32] It was not an unusual occurrence for Lincoln to be seen in public. He was not about to let the threat of death restrict his movement.

Lincoln's longtime and trusted bodyguard Ward Hill Lamon was in Richmond on business the night of April 14. Frustrated by what he perceived as Lincoln's nonchalance about his own safety, Lamon, marshal of the District of Columbia, had sent the president a letter four months before his assassination reminding him to be careful. Lamon intoned, "I regret that you do not appreciate what I have repeatedly said to you in regard to the proper police arrangements connected with your household and your personal safety. You are in danger. . . . And you know, or ought to know, your life is sought after, and will be taken unless you and your friends are cautious."[33] In retrospect, this was good advice that went unheeded.

Abraham and Mary left the White House a little after eight o'clock on the evening of April 14 to pick up their guests Henry R. Rathbone and Clara Harris, both of Albany, New York, at the home of Senator Ira Harris. It was a cloudy night as the Lincoln party made their way to Ford's Theatre and entered the flag-draped state box at approximately eight thirty. Booth's morbid blueprint called for the killing of Lincoln, Vice President Andrew Johnson, and Secretary of State William H. Seward. Five months before his attack, Booth sent a letter to his brother-in-law in which he defended white supremacy. In spelling out his racist ideology, Booth declared, "This country was formed for the *white* not for the black man." And he considered slavery "one of the greatest blessings" of the nation.[34] As Lincoln was taking his place in the presidential box, the would-be assassins were seated at a table in the Herndon House, a boarding house, putting the final touches to their plot.

Booth's plan called for the decapitation of the Washington government to begin at ten fifteen that night. It was after ten o'clock when Booth slipped into the theater and went in search of his target. Once inside the box, Booth pulled his .44 caliber derringer and shot the president. If Booth's fellow conspirators had synchronized their watches, they would have known that he had carried out his part of the plan at the appointed time. The legacy he left "for his fellow white supremacists" was the assassination of the sixteenth president.[35] General Isham N. Haynie, a friend of Lincoln's from Illinois, recorded in his diary that he caught sight of Booth as he made his way to the presidential box and then he "saw the smoke" floating in the air.[36]

When the realization of what had happened fell on the theatergoers, excitement filled the room. The audience jumped to their feet and several hundred rushed toward the place where the crime had occurred. Word also started to circulate that Secretary Seward had been murdered on the same fateful night, causing the mayhem inside the theater to spill into the streets. The pandemonium that had broken out that night on the Potomac River would be fixed in the minds of the theater attendees and Washington residents for years to come. Two physicians rushed to the incapacitated Lincoln and decided to move him to a nearby boarding house, the home of William Petersen.

As the president lay dying and dawn broke over the capital city, Secretary Stanton sent a telegram to John A. Dix, commander of the military district of New York, at 4:44 A.M. "The President continues insensible," he confessed, "and is sinking."[37] Stanton's message made it obvious that Lincoln's condition was hopeless. Word began to spread regarding what had happened to the president, but also of the attack on Seward and his son Frederick. With rain beating down on the Petersen House, the Lincoln devotees were keeping

This glass negative illustration (ca. 1908–19) depicts the assassination of President Lincoln at Ford's Theatre by John Wilkes Booth on the night of April 14, 1865. LC-DIG-npcc-19653, Prints and Photographs Division, Library of Congress.

a vigil inside and Black Washingtonians were doing the same out-side. The scene inside the death chamber left the night watchers emotionally drained. Secretary of the Navy Gideon Welles left the bedside of the dying president for a little fresh air at six o'clock that morning. As Welles walked in the rain, he was stopped by distraught Washingtonians and asked about the patient's condition. Welles recalled, "Intense grief exhibited itself on every countenance when I replied—that the President could survive but a short time. The colored people especially—and there were at this time more of them perhaps than of whites—were painfully affected."[38] Hopelessness knew no bounds as Black and white Americans filled the streets of the capital in search of information about the unprecedented occurrence.

In anticipation of Lincoln's fate, Black Washingtonians were al-ready in a state of mourning. After holding on for nine hours, Lin-coln died at 7:22 A.M. on April 15, 1865, at the age of fifty-six. With his demise, "the chorus of the Union" lost its most powerful and elegant voice. Mary and Abraham's marriage of almost twenty-three years, which at times was tumultuous, was brought to an abrupt and inglorious end by Booth. Mary Lincoln descended into an anguished condition after the nightmarish drama on Tenth Street. The death of Lincoln forever shattered Seward's belief that "assassination is not an American practice or habit, and one so vi-cious and desperate cannot be engrafted into our political system."[39] Three presidents after Lincoln were removed from the highest office in the nation by assassination.

It seemed appropriate that Lincoln had died in a modest board-ing house. After all, he was not born to wealth or refinement, but rather in a log cabin on the Kentucky frontier. The chaplain and Lincoln's private secretary Edward D. Neill remembered his friend as one who was not "artificial or mechanical" and who always had time for those who were poor.[40] Lincoln's lack of ostentatiousness in addition to his accessibility were among his most important at-tributes. A distraught Stanton offered a brief eulogy for his beloved boss. He pronounced the memorable words, "Now he belongs to the ages." Tolling bells and flags blowing in the wind at half-mast

spread throughout Washington and beyond. Soon after the calami-
tous event, the *New Orleans Tribune* called on Black citizens of the
Crescent City to express in public their "grief and sorrow" by wearing mourning badges for thirty days.[41]

The unforgettable scene inside the theater had shocked white
officers and enlisted men of the Union army. Captain Davis E.
Castle of Indiana recorded that the assassination brought about "a
day of mourning" caused by the "bloody deed" of a Southern actor.
Castle maintained that the violent act "was a moment of awful
Excitement."[42] Union soldier William H. Jones of Ohio reflected
on the death of Lincoln in a letter to his wife, Sarah, while in camp
at Selma, Alabama. He wrote, "It is a great loss to our Country at
the present time. Everyone in the army appears to feel very bad
about it."[43] The anonymous author of an 1865 manuscript remembered the event at Ford's Theatre as a "tragedy which resulted in
the murder of President Lincoln."[44] In the North, anger was a common response to the assassination. The members of the Union
League of Hartford, Connecticut, claimed that their "wrath toward
all who participated in the horrid crime" was indisputable.[45] There
was no shortage of sorrow in the immediate hours after the president's death in the city of the dreadful episode.

Expression of unbridled emotion among Black mourners was a
common response of the oppressed and downtrodden race. African
Americans' veneration for Lincoln reached a crescendo after his assassination, prompting them to cease their criticism of him. Lincoln's glacial pace in freeing those in chains and his reluctance to
enroll Black men into the federal army were dismissed. The president's effort to blame the existence of Black Americans for the war,
his tolerance for racial injustice, and his advocacy of colonization
were also overlooked. The abolitionist William Wells Brown
doubtless captured the sentiments of many of his fellow African
Americans regarding the tragic event. "Faults he had; but we forget them all in his death," Brown asserted. "It seemed to us that
God raised this man up to do a great work."[46]

The dreary weather on the day of Lincoln's death seemed an appropriate backdrop for Blacks as they gathered near the White

House in lamentation. Raindrops mixed with tear drops formed an unforgettable image on the faces of those crowded on Pennsylvania Avenue. Black Washingtonians left their communities and ventured into the spring rain to intermingle with those who were dejected. When Mary Jane, the wife of Gideon Welles, asked the hysterical widowed First Lady whom she wanted with her, she answered, "Send for Elizabeth Keckley. I want her just as soon as she can be brought here."[47] When Keckley arrived at the White House, she found a brokenhearted widow in desperate need of a sympathetic shoulder to lean on. As the hearse pulled away from the Petersen House at nine thirty on Saturday morning, a crowd of Black and white mourners accompanied the body to the Presidential Mansion.

The word-of-mouth transmission of the news of the Washington tragedy represented an initial form of mourning. By commiserating with fellow mourners about the crime, an individual did not have to suffer the pain of sorrow alone.[48] Throughout the day, crestfallen people of color continued to gather near the White House, forming "a thick dark ribbon on the walk. The cold rain stitched their backs, but they did not move." A weeping Black man on Pennsylvania Avenue feared that the assassination did not portend well for his race. "If death can come to him," he screamed, "what will happen to us?"[49]

Louisa Jacobs, the daughter of the noted Black abolitionist and author Harriet Jacobs, recorded the reaction of a Black Washingtonian named Old Aunt Sicily who had spent many years in bondage. The day after Lincoln's death, Aunt Sicily said to Louisa, "I can't believe that such a good man is dead. But, child, they can't kill his work. They can't put the chains on me again."[50] For this Lincoln admirer, reenslavement was not an option.

In surveying the homes in the nation's capital, Secretary Welles admitted that he could not ignore the extravagant signs of bereavement on the homes of the affluent. Nonetheless, he acknowledged that "the little black ribbon, or strip of black cloth from the hovel of the poor negro, or the impoverished white is more touching."[51]

Mary Todd Lincoln (1818–82) pictured in mourning attire. After the assassination, she was attended to by her Black confidant Elizabeth Keckley. LC-DIG-ppmsca-52231, Prints and Photographs Division, Library of Congress.

Obviously, fashioning emblems of sorrow was a ubiquitous activity shared by Blacks and whites alike.

It was Easter Sunday when workers began constructing a wooden platform on which Lincoln's casket would rest in the East Room of the White House. The noise reverberating from hammers striking nails was a source of irritation to Mary Lincoln because the sound reminded her of gunfire. The first opportunity for the public to look at the president's body occurred three days after his death. At ten o'clock on the cloudy Tuesday morning of April 18, 1865, the opening of the doors to the Presidential Mansion signaled to the mourners that the viewing could begin. In a *New York Herald* article of April 20, the newspaper stated that "every person moved along on tiptoe, as if fearful of disturbing the long and deep sleep of the" deceased.[52] A Black woman with "sweat drops standing on her ebony brow" held her grandchild above the crowd while in line. Her explanation for lifting the girl was, "I wants dis little chile to see de man who made her free." A reporter witnessed a Black woman who paused at the open coffin, "alternately gazing and sobbing, until at length she was gently reminded by an official" to move on. She stepped aside and continued to weep.[53] An observer who paid attention to the bereaved as they participated in the commemoration noted, "Every class, race and condition of society was represented in the throng of mourners . . . [and] whites and blacks were mingled by the coffin of him to whom humanity was everywhere the same. The most touching exhibitions of sorrow were made by many whose dress marked them as of the poorer classes of society."[54] The more than twenty-five thousand mourners who passed through the East Room represented a mosaic of America.

The modiste Elizabeth Keckley did not have to worry about being rushed when she went to view the body. "I gazed long at the face and turned away with tears in my eyes and a choking sensation in my throat. Ah! never was man so widely mourned before." Keckley remarked that "the whole world bowed their heads in grief when Abraham Lincoln died."[55] Mary Lincoln's confidant had engaged in a bit of exaggeration, because numerous white Southerners were not sad to see him go.

During the public viewing at the White House, the Black surgeon Anderson Ruffin Abbott went there to gaze on the wartime president. The Canadian who received his medical training at the University of Toronto, procured a commission as an acting assistant surgeon with the Union army, which he accepted in June 1863. Upon receiving his orders, he proceeded to a large hospital for African American troops in the District of Columbia. Later he assumed the administrative leadership of the facility as its chief executive. Abbott and Alexander T. Augusta, also a Black surgeon, met Lincoln at a reception at the White House in February 1864. Without an invitation, the two surgeons of the Union army, in full uniform, boldly walked through the presidential doors and mingled with visitors. Abbott recalled that the president's interaction with them was cordial and respectful. He also noted that they were a fascination to some of the guests and the target of indignation by others.[56] When Abbott returned to the White House for the viewing of Lincoln's body in 1865, he remembered looking "upon the pale, cold face of the President as he lay in state in the guests' room ... paralyzed in death."[57]

On Wednesday, April 19, four days after the passing of Lincoln, his funeral took place in the East Room of the White House. According to a newspaper writer, Lincoln's coffin was magnificent and cost about $2,000 to manufacture.[58] Six hundred people, including many dignitaries, attended the funeral. With only a few women in attendance, masculinity was very much on display. One woman who was conspicuously absent from the service was the inconsolable Mary, who remained in the presidential quarters with her son Thomas "Tad" Lincoln. Her firstborn, Robert Todd Lincoln, represented the First Family at the funeral. This was not the first time that Mary was absent for the funeral of an immediate family member. A devastating blow to the Lincolns was the death of their son Eddie on February 1, 1850, at the age of three. Mary most likely did not attend Eddie's funeral, which was held in her home, and she stayed away from his burial. Mary's habit of not attending the funerals of family members would be repeated on future occasions.[59] Prostrated by grief, she was absent at the obsequies and burial of her third son, Willie, who had died in February 1862 at the age of eleven. The convention at that time called for women to avoid attending funerals because of the belief that they were unable to "properly control their emotions."[60] By refusing to participate in or attend any of the funerals, Mary Lincoln was also embracing "the sentimental idea that mourning" was a private practice.[61] Her approach to mourning significantly contrasted with that of many African Americans who were public and demonstrative in their expressions of sorrow.

In Richmond, people of color who were unable to secure black cloth solved that problem with a bit of ingenuity by dipping "floursacks in chimney soot" to create the desired color. Lincoln's burial in Springfield did not go unnoticed in Richmond, as "hundreds of Negroes sat in the pews of the First African Church praying in silence for their deliverer."[62] Their inability to attend the funeral in Illinois had not prevented them from participating in a solemn tribute for the martyred chief. Black workers at a Richmond eatery doled out punishment to a Southern veteran because of his lack of judgment. A reporter recalled that the paroled rebel soldier, while dining at the Ballard House, blurted out that he was "damned glad that Lincoln was dead." Angered by the impolite comment, the Black waiters threw the Confederate diner out of the inn.[63]

San Francisco hosted a ceremony for the president on April 19. Several thousand people watched the commemorative parade as it moved slowly through the city. From the perspective of the city's Black newspaper the *Elevator*, African American mourners constituted one of the most impressive groups in the procession. The editorial made a point of stating that "the colored people made a very fine appearance, and turned out in full force, numbering nearly five hundred men, all well dressed, and looking as well as any portion of the procession." Their dignified behavior, however, was insufficient to protect them from a racial incident during the commemoration in the California city. The funeral was disrupted when a contingent of Irish American soldiers dashed through the parade as African American marchers were crossing from Market Street to Second Street. This incursion caused them to become separated from the rest of the procession. The newspaper referred to this episode as "evidence of disrespect."[64] Regardless of where Black people lived in America, racial animus had a way of finding them.

After the ceremony in the East Room, the relocation of Lincoln's body to the Capitol was next on the agenda. African Americans were both spectators and active participants in the funeral march. The War Department made certain that a regiment of the USCT would be among the military units in the column. Through an assistant adjutant general, Ulysses S. Grant had requested "one of the best regiments of colored troops" from the all-Black Twenty-Fifth Corps to be immediately sent from Petersburg to Washington.[65] General Godfrey Weitzel designated the battle-tested Twenty-Second USCT for this assignment because of their superb skills at soldiering. These volunteers had seen action in the Petersburg and Richmond campaigns. The selected unit arrived in Washington at midday on April 19. The procession started from the White House at two o'clock in the afternoon for the mile-and-a-half walk to the Capitol. The Twenty-Second rested near Pennsylvania Avenue, and when the cortege approached their location the men stepped forward, causing them to occupy a place of honor by marching at the head of the slow-moving funeral procession.[66] This was not the original plan. With the streets and sidewalks jammed with marchers and spectators, the Black soldiers could not reach their place in the line. The parade officials allowed these troops to remain in the advance position in the procession.

The Black regiment's "admirable marching and soldierly bearing was remarked by all," said one reporter, "and formed one of the most prominent features of the occasion."[67] The men of the Twenty-Second considered it an "honor" to have escorted the body of their "beloved late Chief Magistrate and Commander in Chief" from the Presidential Mansion to the Capitol Building.[68] This, however, was not the first time that Black troops, no longer a military oddity of the U.S. Army, had marched in an event in Washington. Four companies of the Forty-Fourth USCT had cherished the opportunity of marching in Lincoln's second inaugural parade forty-five days earlier.

The Washington, D.C., funeral for Abraham Lincoln took place on April 19, 1865. Several thousand African Americans watched the procession from the White House to the Capitol Building, led by the Twenty-Second USCT. LC-USZ62–6935, Prints and Photographs Division, Library of Congress.

Perhaps it was a bit ironic that African Americans occupied both the first and last places in Lincoln's funeral procession. Upon reaching the Capitol, the Veteran Reserve Corps carried the body of their commander in chief into the rotunda to repose in state. An important component in the smooth operation of Lincoln's funeral was the men of the Veteran Reserve Corps, the official pallbearers. This military organization, formerly known as the Invalid Corps, consisted of Union soldiers with limited ability.

During the transport of Lincoln's body to the Capitol, a correspondent for the *New York Tribune* noticed the large number of African Americans lining the streets. He reported, "The colored population, old and young, and all the fifteen thousand that live in the city were reverently awaiting the procession. Dressed in their best, and all even [with] children in arms, wearing badges of mourning, they talked in low tones of him that was gone as the savior of their race, their liberator."[69] The reaction of Blacks along the route also caught the attention of a former enslaved person. To her, it seemed "as if every colored person in the world was there, praying and crying and weeping, falling down on their knees, and bending over until their heads nearly touched the ground, in reverence and grief as the body passed by."[70] It was not unusual for different descriptions of the same event to appear during the war. The first report of the parade quoted here came from the pen of a journalist. The other account was provided by a Black mourner who likely was heartbroken. Their locations along the route might also help to explain the varying observations. Among the most memorable participants in the procession were two hundred Black women. A reporter for the *New Orleans Tribune* described them thusly: "Their heads white with the frosts of age, and dressed in garments exhibiting all hues of the rainbow—some clad in handsome tints, some in mourning, some in red, white and blue calicoes. Some wore handsomely trimmed bonnets, and some, who probably had none to wear, had covered their head with handkerchief. They were followed by a long string of colored urchins. The sight was novel."[71]

The members of Black organizations that participated in the funeral impressed onlookers with their dignified comportment. The

Liberator referred to "the Colored Benevolent Associations, with their banners draped, and their walk and mien the very impersonation of sorrow."[72] Noah Brooks, a young journalist and confidant of the president, recounted the African American participation in the funeral parade of April 19 with these words: "A noticeable feature of the procession was the appearance of the colored societies which brought up the rear, humbly as is their wont. These colored people were out in great numbers as Masons, Odd Fellows, Sons of Temperance, and mutual benefit societies, and a general remark was made upon their respectful and respectable appearance."[73] According to one description, "The first group, forty abreast, was dressed in nocturnal suits, white gloves, tall black hats, and totaled thirty-eight ranks."[74] The Black marchers represented not only themselves but all of Black Washington with elegance.

On Thursday, April 20, 1865, a continuous line of African American mourners passed by the coffin. Sojourner Truth was among the well-known African Americans who paid homage to the martyred president. When she took a glance at Lincoln "cold and still in death," she could not hold back the tears.[75] One contemporary observer noted that African American mourners appeared "like black atoms moving over a sheet of gray paper" while paying their respects.[76] A Black woman named Aunt Vina reflected on her own mortality during the melancholy event. She mused that although Lincoln's earthly journey was over, she "hoped to meet him face to face in Glory, very soon." Despite being "tired, sleepy, and hungry," Aunt Vina stood in line for many hours to get a glimpse of the corpse. As she passed by the coffin, she started to cry "like a newborn baby."[77]

The assassination was a stunning blow not only to people of color but to other Americans as well. Secretary of War Edwin M. Stanton decided to take the funeral to the people by rail. Since the public funeral was under the direction of the War Department, the train proceeded with military precision to Springfield. It was Stanton's intention for the prolonged funeral to leave Americans emotionally drained. To accomplish that goal, Stanton made certain that hundreds of thousands of mourners would have an opportunity to gaze on the face of the stricken leader. The political nature of the funeral cannot be overlooked. Stanton hoped to generate hatred for the South and support for the Republican Party. For many Americans, both Black and white, their brief look at the body served as their tribute to the president. Those along the funeral route were spellbound by the traveling spectacle.

CHAPTER TWO

Slow Ride to Springfield

BECAUSE MARY LINCOLN was burdened with grief, she remained at the White House as the train made its thirteen-day trek across the country in what amounted to the first national funeral in American history. Lincoln's widow was ada-mant that the final resting place for her husband would be Spring-field, Illinois, not Washington, D.C. Mary wanted to forget the unhappy memories associated with the nation's capital. Because Elizabeth Keckley was present to attend to her, Mary was able to stay in residence. The prospect of Mary having to engage with a sea of people along the route for several days in her vulnerable state was more than she could stand. It was not surprising that the widow was a no-show on her husband's funeral train. This was in keeping with her previous actions regarding the death of loved ones. The skeletal remains of Willie accompanied his father on the journey home. It was apparent to the organizers that "no single funeral could possibly accommodate such widespread and overwhelming grief."[1] Before reaching its destination, the train stopped to allow viewings to take place in Baltimore, Harrisburg, Philadelphia, New York, Albany, Buffalo, Cleveland, Columbus, Indianapolis, and Chicago.

Most of the nation's African Americans, including the four mil-lion former bondmen, the people most affected by Lincoln, would not have the opportunity of participating in the funeral. Lincoln's unpopularity in the South, in addition to insufficient rail systems, contributed to the War Department's decision to avoid the defeated Confederate States. During the president's funeral, his body "was

47

considered public property" by African Americans and Northerners.[2] The long, melancholy journey caused many Americans to reflect on Abraham Lincoln's place in both American and world history. As the funeral cortege made its way across the country, several cities patiently waited to participate in the mournful drama.

With the itinerary set, the train, adorned with American flags and a photograph of the president, was ready to begin a circuitous trek of 1,700 miles. On Friday, April 21, a hearse transported Lincoln's body from the Capitol to a waiting nine-car train at the Baltimore & Ohio Railroad Station to start the first leg of the slow ride to Springfield. En route to the depot, the cortege passed in front of two units of Black soldiers. They stood in silence, shedding tears for their commander in chief. At the rear of the railroad station was a building where troops gathered before heading to the front lines. The Eighth U.S. Colored Artillery was having breakfast there when the train prepared to leave the depot. Upon hearing the whistle, the soldiers of the Eighth Regiment fell in line. And as they saluted their chief, "not a dry eye" could be found among them.[3] The time had come for Lincoln to make his final exit from the city on the Potomac River and embark on an epic journey. Military, political, and religious leaders had given Lincoln a dignified and memorable funeral in Washington. Since the national crisis kept Secretary Edwin M. Stanton there, he appointed Edward D. Townsend, assistant adjutant general of the U.S. Army, to act on his behalf while accompanying Lincoln's body to Illinois.

The nostalgic nature of the two-week trip was obvious when the planners scheduled the train to travel precisely the same route that brought Lincoln to Washington in 1861 to begin his term as the sixteenth president of the United States. By the time the nation's capital had faded from sight, the train was preparing to make its first stop in Baltimore. The city's reception of the dead president was very different from the treatment that Lincoln received there in 1861. At that time, the city was home to many individuals who sympathized with the secessionists. Unlike during his entry into Baltimore four years earlier, which was a clandestine affair because of death threats, on this occasion the city received Lincoln with enthusiasm and reverence.

By dawn on Friday, April 21, 1865, Baltimore, the largest city in the South, was crowded with spectators waiting for the train to arrive at the Camden Street Station. The hearse that transported Lincoln's body was almost completely made of glass, which allowed those waiting along the procession to clearly see the coffin. The Committee on Arrangements of Baltimore placed African Americans at the rear of the parade, a practice that would be repeated throughout the journey. That afternoon, Secretary Stanton received a telegram from General Townsend informing him that the streets of Baltimore were packed mainly with "laboring classes, white and black," who were visibly distraught during the "very imposing" ceremonies.[4] With the opening of the coffin in the rotunda of the Mercantile Exchange Building, the people of Baltimore were the first to bid farewell to Lincoln along the funeral route. At Baltimore, "the casket was opened down to the waist, so as to display the face and bust to the" tens of thousands of mourners.[5]

The Black Baltimoreans could not contain their effusion of sadness. One writer claimed, "Nowhere were the manifestations of grief more impressive than at Baltimore, and especially from the negroes. Their coarse, homely features were convulsed with grief they could not control, and sobs, cries, and tears told how deeply they mourned their deliverer."[6] An editorial in the *Weekly Anglo-African* published in New York City summed up the feelings of the Black population in Baltimore, stating that the "awful suddenness" of Lincoln's death, "coupled with its utter fiendishness, has overwhelmed us, as it has the nation at large."[7] A writer for the *New York Tribune* reported on a fascinating scene in Baltimore:

> Let not the reader imagine this an overdrawn picture—it is literally truthful, could not be oversketched in words. White and black stood side by side in the rain and the mud, with eyes strained upon that coffin, with eyes running over, and with clasped hands, and with faces all drawn and distorted or set

in marble fixedness. White and black leaned forth from the same windows; the well-dressed and the shabby in the same doorway, and there seemed to be no consciousness of any difference of color or disparity of station.[8]

Baltimore was not immune from racial division and secessionist dogma. The journalist was perhaps carried away with a bit of hyperbole. His favorable impression of race relations contradicted the reality of life for Blacks in Baltimore.

The closing of the lid at two thirty in the afternoon signaled that the time had come for the journey to continue. The funeral caravan pulled away from the depot of the Northern Central Railway Company with Harrisburg, Pennsylvania, as its destination. A downpour accompanied by lightning and thunder greeted the procession on rails in Harrisburg at eight o'clock on the evening of April 21. There, heavy rain caused the city officials to cancel the ceremony that had been planned for the train's arrival. Despite the inclement weather, citizens lined the streets and followed the coffin to the state capitol. As in the previous practice, the "colored citizens" brought up the rear. Mourners turned out in large numbers to view the president in the Hall of Representatives.[9]

Lincoln's train arrived in Philadelphia, the second-largest city in America, a few minutes before five o'clock in the afternoon on Saturday, April 22. An impressive gathering of nearly five hundred thousand, which included many African Americans, poured into the downtown streets of the City of Brotherly Love. Sprinkled among the mourners were Civil War veterans whose missing limbs reminded Philadelphians of the brutal nature of the conflict. They came to view the remains of the man who had sent them to distant battlefields across the land. Among the soldiers representing the U.S. Army in the procession as it made its way from the Broad Street Depot to Independence Hall were members of the Twenty-Fourth USCT. There were also several African American civic organizations in the parade, such as Masonic lodges, Odd Fellows, and the Delmonico Benevolent Association. The members of these groups were all dressed in black and wore mourning badges.[10] Once the coffin had been placed inside the historic building, the president's head rested a short distance from the Liberty Bell. The scene of the desolate waiting in long lines to take a brief look at the body was repeated in city after city. A newspaper reported that "colored men and women were liberally sprinkled along the line." For an elderly Black woman, it was worth the wait to gaze for a moment at the body. As she approached the catafalque to say goodbye, tears covered "her withered cheeks." She cried, "Oh, Abraham Lincoln; Oh! he is dead; he is dead." The editorial concluded that the "sympathy and love expressed by this poor woman found a response in every heart."[11] Another Black woman went to Independence Hall with a homemade "wreath of evergreen" to display "at the head, or at the feet, or somewhere near the beloved remains" of Lincoln. The Black mourner's "tribute was . . . emblematic of the everlasting remembrance in which the name of Abraham Lincoln would be held in all time to come."[12]

The Black Philadelphia resident Emilie Davis kept diaries during the Civil War in which she recorded many of the momentous events of those tragic years. Davis worked as a domestic servant and was a member of the Ladies' Union Association, a support group for African American soldiers. On Saturday, April 15, Davis recorded her reaction to Lincoln's death in her diary. She wrote, "Very sad newes was received this morning of the murder of the President the city is in deep mourning." Five days later, Davis's observation led her to remark that "everything assumes a solemn aspect the streets look mournful." After witnessing the procession on April 22, Davis stated, "It was the gravest funeral i ever saw." Upon viewing the body, Davis recalled that "it was certainly a sight worth seeing."[13] Before closing the coffin, Charles Brown, a Washington physician and embalmer, brushed away the dust that had collected on Lincoln's face. The waiting hearse took the casket to the Trenton Railroad Depot for departure. On Monday, April 24, at four o'clock in the morning, the funeral train was bound for New York City. An African American who fixed his eyes on the train as it wound its way through Lancaster, Pennsylvania, commented that "he was crucified for us."[14] At least to this mourner, Lincoln had sacrificed his life for the liberation of the downtrodden race.

The rolling funeral arrived on the New Jersey side of the Hudson River six hours later to thousands of waiting visitors. Upon its arrival at the Camden and Amboy Railroad Depot, the Veteran Reserve Corps lifted the coffin from the train and deposited it in a waiting hearse. Six gray horses conveyed it to the ferryboat *Jersey City* for delivery to Manhattan. This short trip across the river was the first of two boat rides that the president's procession would make during its journey to Springfield. Each of the sixteen gray horses that pulled Lincoln's body to city hall was led by a Black groom. The glass-plated carriage allowed the multitude along the way a clear look at the casket. Although the embalmer traveled with the body and plied his craft, he could not prevent the deterioration of the deceased. In New York City, "the old and the young, the rich and the poor, without distinction of color or sex," passed quietly by the coffin.[15] For several days, America's largest city suffered from a paralysis of despair. Businesses closed and the financial district was void of activity.

In anticipation of the stop in New York, a committee of influential Blacks requested a place in the procession for about five thousand members of their race from the Common Council, controlled by Democrats. The council crushed their hope of joining the solemnities when it announced that they would be barred from appearing in the march. The city government's controversial order declared, "No Negroes marching!—and Positively no black people in our procession." Black New Yorkers strained their imagination to understand how Lincoln's horse had been allowed to march in Washington, but they would be denied an opportunity of marching in the Empire City.[16] Council members based their decision on the presumption that Blacks would cause trouble in retaliation for the deaths of their brethren during the draft riot in July 1863. During the disturbance, white mobs had descended on Blacks, killing and injuring several dozens of them. The violence also claimed the Colored Orphans Asylum when it was burned to the ground.[17]

For the moment, the officials had refused African Americans the satisfaction of participating in the procession. James W. C. Pennington of New York, a former enslaved person, Presbyterian minister, and prominent leader of the Colored Convention Movement, criticized the Common Council in a letter to the *Weekly Anglo-African*. Reverend Pennington said that "the spirit that would exclude colored men from the President's funeral, is the same that murdered him, from whomsoever it may come."[18] Pennington, in calling for the inclusion of Blacks in the solemn event, was also concerned about racial violence. He sent a letter to the editor of the *New York Tribune* on April 21, 1865, in which he detailed an unpleasant incident as an illustration of the racial hatred found in the municipality.

As Pennington was returning home from preaching at the African Methodist Episcopal Church in Brooklyn, three young white men approached him as he walked on Sixth Avenue. One of the men, while staring at the mourning badge on Pennington's chest, remarked, "Ain't you sorry your father Abe Lincoln is dead!" Another shouted, "Hurrah for Jeff. Davis." And the third threatened to "shoot" him. "It is well for the American to know that the murder of Mr. Lincoln has intensified the feeling of barbarism toward us," the reverend said, "and if not checked, will result as heretofore." Pennington summed up his missive with a bit of advice for the city. "A single word from each press, and pulpit, and platform," he counseled, "will abate this street nuisance."[19]

Reverend Pennington was not alone among African American leaders who called attention to the plight of people of color following the death of Lincoln. On May 9, 1865, the Black abolitionist Charles Lenox Remond of Massachusetts delivered a speech at the annual meeting of the American Anti-Slavery Society in New York City. A little more than a year earlier, in 1864, Remond, along with three other Black men, had attended a New Year's Day reception at the White House. Remond, who was well known in the arena of social activism, was convinced that many white Americans did not comprehend the exasperation of Black people in the country. "I do assume here that it is utterly impossible for any of our white friends," he proclaimed, "however much they may have tried, fully to understand the Black man's case in this nation." Before closing, Remond reminded the conclave of the "hatred of the colored man in the North."[20] Racial oppression remained a fact of life for African Americans in New York and other places before, during, and after the Civil War.

New York's decision to deny members of the USCT a place in the column seemed particularly appalling to the city's Black community. Among the African Americans who were disappointed by the action of the Common Council was Reverend John Sella Martin, abolitionist and pastor of the First Colored Presbyterian Church of New York. The refusal to allow Black soldiers to march in the procession was clear evidence to him that people of color still had many hurdles to cross. The prominent preacher made an eloquent appeal to the city government to rescind the prohibition. Martin maintained that if Lincoln had "been consulted he would have urged, as a dying request, that the representatives of the race which had come to the nation's rescue in the hour of peril, and which he had lifted by the most solemn official acts to the dignity of citizens and defenders of the Union, should be allowed the honor of following his remains to the grave."[21] The council's ban was discussed at a meeting at Shiloh Church where Blacks indicated their willingness to participate in the funeral in defiance of the restriction.

A New York journal denounced the ignominy of the Common Council when it declared that Lincoln "was venerated by the whole colored population with a peculiar degree of feeling; they looked upon him as the liberator of their race; and now . . . to be refused the privilege of paying respect to his remains is mortifying and humiliating."[22] A letter appearing in the *New York Tribune* from a Black resident also focused on the exclusionary edict. "The Common Council of this city have refused to allow a place for our respectable Colored Societies and citizens in the procession," he wrote, "to be held in honor of him whose death we all so deeply lament."[23] The Black citizens of New York were not silent but instead vigorously protested the city's injustice.

The intransigence of the Common Council gave way to the intervention of the War Department. When word of the council's directive reached Secretary Stanton, he took decisive action. Assistant Secretary of War Charles Anderson Dana sent a telegram from Washington to General John A. Dix, commander of the military district of New York. The telegraphic note inveighed, "It is the desire of the Secretary of War that no discrimination respecting color should be exercised in admitting persons to the general procession tomorrow. In this city a black regiment formed part of the funeral escort."[24] When the secretary of war invalidated the city's racist decree, the Common Council lifted the prohibition against Blacks marching in the cavalcade. Assuming the role of town crier, the newspapers informed the city that Black citizens and their organizations would be permitted to march. African Americans who intended to participate in the procession had to be in place by noon on April 24, and they also had to provide their own marshals for supervision.[25] The cortege, which initially excluded Black citizens of the metropolis, was an embarrassment to some city leaders.

Once they could participate, approximately two hundred well-dressed African Americans brought up the rear of the grand parade. This was a significant decrease from the original number of five thousand. The fear of retaliation from angry whites caused thousands of Blacks not to take part in the procession. To prevent any trouble, a contingent of police officers protected the Black marchers. Four men carried a banner which read, "Abraham Lincoln, our Emancipator." And on the reverse side appeared the following statement: "To Millions of Bondsmen he Liberty Gave."[26] As the funeral procession came upon a brothel on Canal Street, many of "the windows were crowded with the sad faces of negroes and mulattoes," the *New York Tribune* reported, "most of whom were ladies." The ceremony was frequently punctuated with expressions of sorrow from the crowd. When the parade reached the corner of West Broadway and Canal Street, "an old negress was weeping very violently," proclaiming, "He died for me! he died for me! God bless him!"[27] For her, like so many other Black mourners, Lincoln's death was personal.

This illustration of Lincoln's funeral in New York is based on a
photograph taken by Mathew Brady that appeared in *Harper's Weekly*
on May 13, 1865. As was the custom in all the cities on the route to
Springfield, Black groomsmen led the horses pulling the coffin.
Courtesy of Wikimedia Commons.

The Black soldiers who marched in the procession "were greeted with every mark of respect and consideration" from the spectators along Fifth Avenue.[28] The inclusion of a few hundred Blacks in the cortege was not without controversy. Some of New York City's aldermen protested their presence by refusing to participate in a march that included Black residents.[29] In total, more than three hundred thousand mostly white spectators turned out to watch the procession. When the authorities closed the doors to city hall shortly before noon on April 25, tens of thousands of mourners were in line waiting to pay their respects. At two o'clock that afternoon, the official pallbearers loaded Lincoln's coffin into the hearse for the return to the Hudson River Railroad Station. Following the unforgettable farewell in New York, the greatest commemoration in the history of the nation up to that time, the train continued to Springfield. At four fifteen in the afternoon, the whistle sounded, indicating the departure for Albany, New York. Although the Empire City had hosted several large and impressive funerals and parades, none of them compared "either in size or in grandeur" to the mournful pageant for the sixteenth president.[30]

A group of Black New Yorkers responded to the disenchantment caused by the Common Council by organizing a tribute in honor of the slain leader at Cooper Union. Mostly African Americans turned out on June 1, 1865, to hear the keynote speaker, Frederick Douglass, eulogize his friend. That date coincided with President Andrew Johnson's proclamation designating June 1 as a day of national humiliation, ending the period of official mourning. Johnson encouraged his fellow Americans to go to their places of worship to commemorate the life of Lincoln. Douglass began by telling the assembly, "The attempt to exclude colored people from his funeral procession in New York—was one of the most disgraceful; and sickening manifestations of moral emptiness, ever exhibited by any nation of people professing to be civilized."[31] He posited that Lincoln was "emphatically the black man's President: the first to show any respect for their rights as men."[32] Douglass praised the martyred man as "one of the very few white Americans who could converse with a negro without anything like condescension, and without in anywise reminding him of the unpopularity of his color."[33]

During his Cooper Union speech, Douglass referred to a memorable scene that "occurred at the gate of the Presidential mansion. A colored woman standing at the gate weeping, was asked the cause of her tears; 'Oh! Sir,' she said 'we have lost our Moses.' But said the gentleman, 'the Lord will send you another.' 'That may be,' said the weeping woman, 'but Ah! we had him.'" Douglass affirmed that Black Americans had made significant progress under Lincoln's leadership. He reminisced, "Under his rule, they saw millions of their brethren proclaimed free and invested with the right to defend their freedom. Under his rule, they saw the Confederate states . . . broken to pieces, overpowered, conquered, shattered to fragments, ground to powder, and swept from the face of existence." Douglass brought his Cooper Union address to a close by acknowledging that "Mr Lincoln soon outgrew his colonization ideas and schemes—and came to look upon the Blackman as an American citizen."[34] After Lincoln's death, some Americans, including Blacks, continued to promote colonization as a solution to the problem of race in the nation. Douglass was optimistic that his people in the not-too-distant future would be the beneficiaries of civil and political rights.

The topic of race in American life found a perch in city after city along the funeral route. The *New York Tribune* had reported that a modicum of racial tolerance existed among Black and white mourners in Baltimore. When juxtaposing Baltimore to New York City, a different portrait emerged. Municipal authorities in New York stoked the flames of racial animosity. Violence against Black individuals, combined with the city's exclusionary edict, revealed that it was not an oasis of racial harmony. The Black citizens of New York sought redress through protest, a time-honored American tradition. The funeral in New York would be remembered not only for its size but also for the city's effort to preclude the participation of African Americans.

After traveling 140 miles, the train pulled into the Hudson River Railroad Depot of East Albany at eleven o'clock on the night of

April 25. From there, a ferry took the body to the west side of the Hudson River. Thousands of people turned out along the banks to watch the unfolding event. Upon reaching land, the procession formed and made its way to the Assembly Chamber, where the body would lie in state. The removal of the casket lid at one o'clock in the morning on April 26 exposed the president's remains to the bereaved. With every new stop the body revealed more marks of decay. In Albany, the *New York Times* estimated that fifty thousand people turned out to see "the placid features" of Lincoln.[35] As the mourners streamed pass the coffin, they "looked sorrowfully on the cold and sacred clay with throbbing hearts. They felt in their inmost souls as if they had lost their dearest household treasure."[36] Louise Coffin Smith of Albany documented the reaction of a Black female upon seeing the corpse. Smith wrote, "An old colored woman just ahead of us attempted to kiss him, saying between sobs, 'we have lost our best friend.' Soldiers hurried her on."[37]

Two notable episodes of the war occurred on Wednesday, April 26; one in North Carolina and the other in Virginia. On that date, near Durham Station in North Carolina, General Joseph E. Johnston handed over his army of thirty thousand men to General William T. Sherman based on the same terms that General Ulysses S. Grant had given to Robert E. Lee seventeen days earlier at Appomattox. Speaking a few weeks later as a victorious military leader, Sherman asserted that the United States had no alternative but to completely subdue its adversary. He boasted that "as long as the enemy was defiant, no mountains, no rivers, nor swamps nor hunger, nor cold had checked us."[38] As the funeral train was closing in on Albany, federal soldiers were closing in on John Wilkes Booth in Virginia. As Lincoln's caravan made its way across the country, Booth was the object of a huge manhunt. In Virginia, he and David Herold were found by Union soldiers, holed up in a tobacco barn on Richard H. Garrett's farm less than eighty miles from the scene of the assassination. Herold was captured and Booth was shot and killed on the morning of April 26 by Sergeant Boston Corbett. Two weeks later, Lincoln's assassin would have turned twenty-seven years old.

The traveling special left Albany on Wednesday, April 26, at four o'clock in the afternoon and pulled into the Exchange Street Depot in Buffalo at seven o'clock the next morning. In anticipation of the arrival of the funeral train, the people of Buffalo had decorated their homes in the habiliments of mourning. A crowd escorted Lincoln's body to St. James Hall in the Young Men's Association building, where the remains were displayed. Once inside the hall, mourners shuffled by the catafalque to take a glimpse of the man from the Prairie State. Among the grievers were men and women from Canada.

Black Canadians, many of whom had settled in Buxton, Canada, having fled from slavery in the United States, shared the emotions of their brethren to the south upon learning of the death of "Ole Massa Lincoln."[39] When word of Lincoln's death drifted across the border, African Canadians could not hold back their tears. They admired Lincoln because of his commitment to honesty. They not only held commemorative services in his honor, but many wanted to gaze upon his face. The proximity of Buffalo to the Canadian line allowed them to carry out their wish. When the funeral train arrived at Buffalo, "long lines of Canadians crossed the bridge to share in the sorrow of their neighbors."[40] Shortly after ten o'clock on the night of April 27, the train left Buffalo for Cleveland, Ohio.

When the train conveying Lincoln's body reached Wickliffe, a short distance from Cleveland, Governor John Brough, General Joseph Hooker, and Senator John Sherman were among the dignitaries who went aboard. The mournful cortege arrived in the city on the morning of April 28 amid a steady rain, which convinced Clevelanders that heaven was weeping for the man from Illinois. In Cleveland, six white horses each attended by a Black groom drew the hearse from Euclid Station to Public Square. Black groups were among the organizations that joined in the procession, which escorted Lincoln's body to the bier. Eureka Lodge No. 14 represented the Black Masons of the city. Also participating was Lodge No. 1188 of the Grand United Order of Odd Fellows. They displayed a banner that read, "We mourn for Abraham Lincoln, the True Friend of Liberty." The Colored Equal Rights League of Cleveland marched behind the Odd Fellows.[41] With several days to organize the activities, the Cleveland Committee of Arrangements decided to stage the viewing outside because of the lack of a suitable building to accommodate the swarm of people. Regardless of the number of mourners, an open-air funeral could accommodate them all. Only in Cleveland were ceremonies held out-of-doors. The inclement weather did not discourage the public from coming to see the body.

Once the casket was resting on the platform, a delegation of women from the Soldiers' Aid Society of Northern Ohio decorated the box with flowers. Also taking part in the ceremony was the Colored Soldiers' Aid Society. The Black women "offered an admirably arranged wreath of white flowers, which was placed near the head of the coffin at its side."[42] Lincoln was still on the mind of the Colored Soldiers' Aid Society when they met in August 1865. The relief organization presented "a richly engraved portrait" of Lincoln to Mary Parker, the outgoing president of the group. In accepting the gift, Parker said that the members "loved the illustrious dead," who had "fallen by the hands of a cowardly assassin."[43] Although the war was over, the women agreed not to disband but to continue providing aid to Black soldiers.

In Cleveland, thousands quietly and reverently passed by the bier. One estimate claimed that 180 people per minute filed by the coffin, totaling more than 10,000 an hour. In death the notion that Lincoln was a mystical person held sway among some Black Americans. When a former enslaved person announced a desire to see the body, another fellow African American disparaged the idea: "No man see Linkum. Linkum walks as Jesus walk—no man see Linkum."[44] When the clock struck ten o'clock that night the embalmer closed the coffin, bringing the funeral in Cleveland to an end.

The train reached Ohio's capital city of Columbus at seven thirty on the morning of Saturday, April 29, to the sound of muffled bells and a large crowd of mourners who had gathered near the Union Station Depot. As the parade was moving from the depot to the statehouse, the Black Masons and the Colored Benevolent Association brought up the rear. The African American organizations left a lasting impression on the bystanders because of their somber and respectful demeanor.[45] An editorial in the *Daily Ohio Statesman* reported that the citizens of Columbus were crushed by what had happened to the president. "There was accompanying the procession and the solemn exercises of the day," the writer said, "deep and heart-felt grief that pervaded every bosom and pierced all hearts."[46] The pallbearers positioned the coffin in the rotunda of the statehouse in a way that allowed every onlooker a close view. A Columbus newspaper reported that throughout the day, Black and white citizens of all ages passed by the bier.[47] As the train moved across the land, complaints from some white Southerners about the extravagant pageant were increasing in volume and frequency. They were certain that the country's "preoccupation with the mortal remains of Abraham Lincoln" amounted to nothing more than "a vulgar exhibition . . . of a decaying mummy."[48] It should be noted that not all whites of the Confederacy were anti-Lincolnites.

The procession on rails departed from Columbus on the evening of April 29, and the next morning at seven o'clock, after an eleven-hour trip, it pulled into Indianapolis. This was the fourth state capital to host the funeral since its departure from Washington. Lincoln was back in the state where he had spent several years as a young man. The severe weather forced the cancellation of the planned procession through the streets of Indianapolis. The train was greeted there by countless mourners and the firing of a cannon. The hearse carrying the former Indiana citizen was delivered to the statehouse by eight white horses. With the opening of the doors to the statehouse at nine o'clock that morning, Black and white men, women, and children went to view the body. The Black Masons of Indianapolis also paid their respects to the president.[49] The Black community added to the pageantry of the procession by carrying a huge banner of Lincoln's presidential decree of January 1, 1863. In addition to a replica of the Emancipation Proclamation, the mourners carried signs that read, "Colored Men, always Loyal," "Lincoln, Martyr of Liberty," "He lives in our Memories," and "Slavery is Dead."[50] The funeral train left Indianapolis at midnight on May 1, with Chicago as its next stop.

Many Black residents were among the throngs who had assembled at the depot at Lake Park in Chicago to witness the train's arrival. The hearse drawn by "ten black horses, each attended by a colored groom dressed in black," made its way to the Cook County Court House.[51] Schuyler Colfax, the Republican Speaker of the House from Indiana, delivered a speech on May 1 in Bryan Hall to prepare the citizens for the funeral services that would take place in Chicago. Colfax, who was a friend of the deceased, told the audience that Lincoln "live[d] in the grateful hearts of the dark-browed race he lifted from under the heel of the oppressor to the dignity of freedom and manhood."[52] To Colfax, the Emancipation Proclamation was a historic moment for both Lincoln and African Americans.

Leaders of civic organizations, city officials, politicians, and members of the judiciary were among the participants in the parade. The march also included about four hundred African Americans, some of whom displayed banners stating, "We mourn our loss," and "Rest in peace, with a nation's tears."[53] A reporter for the *Christian Recorder* named Ruth chronicled the role of people of color in the Chicago funeral. According to the journalist, the funeral was one of "grandeur," and "the colored citizens turned out in full force, and were well received." Ruth also noted that the procession was void of any derogatory comments aimed at the Black participants.[54]

Lincoln had been dead for more than two weeks by the time the funeral extravaganza reached the largest city in Illinois. A journalist for the *Chicago Tribune* reported that "the high and the low, the rich and the poor, the learned and the unlearned, native and foreign born, white and black, old and young, male and female, have wept at his tomb."[55] When the pallbearers carried Lincoln's body from the courthouse on the morning of May 2, the somber event was approaching an end. The streets were lined with thousands of spectators as the procession passed by on its way to the Chicago and Alton Railway Station to begin the final leg of the journey. The Chicago Citizens' Committee of One Hundred made certain that a Black person was among the delegation that would accompany Lincoln to Springfield. That honor went to the abolitionist and civil rights advocate John Jones, who had settled in Chicago in the 1840s. The selection of Jones was a step in the direction of racial harmony in Chicago. After a two-hundred-mile ride, the train pulled into Springfield.

Secretary Stanton received a telegram from General Townsend informing him that the cortege had arrived in Lincoln's hometown at the Chicago, Alton, and St. Louis Railway Station "without accident at 8:40" on the morning of May 3.[56] Since rail travel in the middle of the nineteenth century was problematic at best, this was a major accomplishment. The train's arrival in the capital city of Illinois nearly on time was a testimony to exceptional planning. The burial the next day would be the final act of the three-week-long drama. After waiting several days, it was Springfield's turn to say goodbye to the president. The procession to the statehouse included citizens of color. As the hearse made its way through the streets, it was obvious that the Springfield Committee of Reception had done its job of preparing the city for the funeral. A portrait of Lincoln hung from the door of his law office. Many houses and businesses were decorated with emblems of mourning, including the president's home.

The casket rested on the catafalque in Representatives Hall in the statehouse, the spot where Lincoln had given his "House Divided" speech seven years earlier. The American flag at half-mast atop the dome of the capitol building was also a visible sign of a city in mourning. During the twenty-four hours of public viewing, a steady flow of mourners visited the statehouse. These were the last people to see Lincoln during the three-week-long grandiose funeral. The closing of the coffin at ten o'clock on Thursday morning, May 4, brought the viewing to an end.

At noon, with the statehouse as a backdrop, Lincoln's friends and associates made their way to Oak Ridge Cemetery, a burial ground known for its beauty. The procession included governors, members of Congress and the Illinois state legislature, military officers, and Black Freemasons and Odd Fellows. A horde of thousands had gathered at the cemetery to await the arrival of the president's body. The two-mile funeral procession, which was under

Abraham Lincoln's draped home in Springfield with Black ministers Henry Brown (*left*) and William C. Trevan (*right*) standing by Lincoln's horse Old Robin, which was also covered for mourning, on May 4, 1865. LC-DIG-ppmsca-52175, Prints and Photographs Division, Library of Congress.

the direction of General Hooker, reached the burial site at one o'clock that afternoon. Lincoln had interacted with some Black residents of Springfield through his law practice and their work as domestics for his family. Henry Brown, a Black preacher, previously had worked as a handyman for the decedent. William C. Trevan, who was also a man of the cloth, marched along with Brown behind the hearse with Old Robin, Lincoln's horse.

Another Black resident of Springfield with whom Lincoln had a personal relationship was his barber, William de Fleurville. Their friendship lasted more than thirty years. Fleurville sent Lincoln a letter in December 1863, to offer his condolences for the death of his son, Willie and to thank him for his support of Black people. He closed the letter to his friend by telling him that he looked forward to the day "When the Rebellion shall be put down."[57] When violence claimed Lincoln, the town's barber carried the weight of gloom with him until his own death in 1868. Fleurville's granddaughter was certain that he never got over Lincoln's assassination, which robbed him of his "high spirits."[58] Fleurville passed up the opportunity to march in the funeral procession with Lincoln's longtime friends at the head of the parade and instead decided to walk at the back of the line in solidarity with the other Black mourners.

Blacks and whites lining the streets in Springfield wept as Lincoln was borne to his limestone tomb; many of them wore a piece of black crepe. Eight Black men led the horses that pulled the hearse to the graveyard. The symbolism of the moment was not lost on African Americans. After all, Lincoln had played a role in leading Blacks out of the darkness of slavery. Many Black people had come to Springfield to say goodbye to the city's best-known resident. In keeping with the practice at other stops, people of color were last in line. Their placement in the line did not concern them. What they valued most was the opportunity to honor the man whom they had lauded as "the benefactor" of their race.[59] However, by the time the Black marchers reached the cemetery, the service was over.

On Thursday afternoon, May 4, 1865, the vault at Oak Ridge Cemetery received Lincoln's body. The next day, the train, no longer carrying its famous passenger, left Springfield without fanfare

The businessman William de Fleurville (1807–68), also known
as Billy the Barber, of Springfield, was Abraham Lincoln's best
Black friend. Like many African Americans, he was deeply hurt
by the assassination. Courtesy of the Abraham Lincoln
Presidential Library and Museum.

or ceremony for the return trip to Washington, D.C. Federal, state, and municipal officials had played important roles to ensure the success of the funeral in the cities it visited. In 1874, the Springfield Zouaves, an African American militia company, took part in the ceremony accompanying President Grant's unveiling of a monument to Lincoln in Oak Ridge Cemetery.[60]

By the time Lincoln's body had been deposited at Oak Ridge Cemetery, millions of people had participated in the historic funeral through private or public displays of mourning. At least one million people viewed Lincoln's body. As the funeral traveled through cities, towns, and villages, disconsolate citizens paused to honor the martyred president. The ceremonies that occurred in the designated cities were conducted by the Committees on Arrangements in a professional manner. From the first stop to the last, funeral planning committees maintained the racial protocol of the mid-nineteenth century by placing Black participants in the processions at the rear. The only exception was Washington, D.C., where Blacks marched at both the front and rear of the funeral parade. Once the majestic funeral was over, African Americans could only imagine what might have been if Lincoln had not been assassinated. Lincoln on many occasions raised his voice in opposition to slavery, and when the time was right, he used the power of the pen to change the course of human history.

CHAPTER THREE

The Emancipator and the Emancipated

ABRAHAM LINCOLN WAS one of many Americans who expressed discontent with slavery, the greatest moral sin in the nation's history. In March 1859, he told a group of Republicans in Chicago that "there is an absolute wrong in the institution of slavery."[1] All the problems associated with the diabolical system were there to greet Lincoln when he entered the White House in 1861. Lincoln undoubtedly knew that slavery would complicate his presidency even before his inauguration.

One aspect of slavery on which Lincoln attempted to walk a political tightrope was his decision to countermand the emancipation edicts of the generals who sought to free the enslaved people under their jurisdiction. In addition to other cases, Lincoln reversed the emancipation edict of General John C. Frémont, commander of the Union forces in Missouri in 1861. He told Frémont's wife, Jessie Benton Frémont, in a meeting with her at the White House that "the General should never have dragged the Negro into the war. It is a war for a great national object and the Negro has nothing to do with it."[2] At the start of the conflict, the president was in step with many of his contemporaries on the idea that the Civil War was a white man's war. Lincoln was willing to grapple with the political backlash resulting from his revocation order. The president's decision produced disappointment among Northerners, abolitionists, and Black leaders. Frederick Douglass criticized the Lincoln administration for committing a huge mistake. Reverend Henry McNeal Turner of South Carolina, chaplain of the First United

69

States Colored Troops (USCT), was also disillusioned with Lincoln's declaration to reverse the freedom orders of his military leaders. Reverend Turner averred that the president had "hardened his heart" toward emancipation.[3]

Lincoln believed that emancipation was the responsibility of the commander in chief of the army and navy. To that end, in April 1862, he signed a bill abolishing slavery in the District of Columbia. Although the new law did not affect the vast majority of the enslaved race, it did give relief to those in bondage in the nation's capital. Black abolitionist and newspaper editor Philip A. Bell criticized Lincoln for not ending slavery everywhere. In mid-June 1862, he stated that the federal government was "pursuing a course detrimental to the best interests of the country and encouraging the Rebels in their efforts to overthrow the Union, and perpetuate slavery."[4]

The approach Lincoln took on the slavery question was to work with several groups, including Radical Republicans and abolitionists. The driving force behind emancipation was Lincoln, not any political, social, religious, or humanitarian group. A task of that magnitude was beyond their capabilities.[5] It was a well-established fact that enslaved men, women, and children had been liberating themselves by running away during the antebellum period, and that trend continued after the outbreak of hostilities. Many scholars of the Civil War era agree that emancipation was a tortuous and complicated process. After months of hesitancy, which produced disenchantment among Lincoln's critics, he finally essayed a powerful strike against the peculiar institution.

On January 1, 1863, President Abraham Lincoln gave the nation and the world the Emancipation Proclamation. He was certain that freeing those in shackles was the work of Almighty God. Another occasion in which Lincoln's belief in a Supreme Being was on display was at an event at the White House in 1864. On September 7, a delegation of Black men from Baltimore, which included Bishop Alexander W. Wayman of the African Methodist Episcopal Church, presented an elegant Bible to Lincoln. The gift was an

Emancipated African Americans celebrating a day of jubilee in an unidentified plantation house in 1865. LC-DIG-ppmsca-10978, Prints and Photographs Division, Library of Congress.

expression of gratitude to the president for the role he had played in the emancipation of their race. In accepting the Bible, Lincoln told the group that he believed "that all mankind should be free" and that the Bible "is the best gift God has given to man."[6]

When Lincoln issued the emancipation decree, free Black people and those in bondage elevated him to the status of a messiah. With the benefit of hindsight, it is also apparent that the Emancipation Proclamation was the catalyst for Lincoln's becoming a martyr for freedom. The president's document of freedom was monumental because this was the first time that the U.S. government had made a commitment to eliminating the inhumane institution instead of merely containing it.[7]

Lincoln issued the Emancipation Proclamation on his authority as commander in chief. It was also a war measure designed to create confusion in the South and to prevent England and France from giving diplomatic recognition to the rebellious states. Notwithstanding this, the limitations of the document were obvious. The proclamation left slavery intact in the loyal border states and in those parts of the Confederacy not in rebellion against the federal government. Freedom without suffrage left countless in the Black community disillusioned. The proclamation included a historic provision that called for the enlistment of men of African descent. Their enrollment in the military changed the war in a mighty way.

Frederick Douglass was elated when Lincoln's declaration went into effect. Douglass hinted that it was "the greatest event of our nation's history if not the greatest event of the century."[8] Hezekiah Ford Douglas's critical assessment of his fellow Illinoisan was commonplace before and during the war. However, he started to moderate his opinion of Lincoln after the proclamation. Douglas, in a letter to Frederick Douglass on January 8, 1863, had kind words for the president. He told the abolitionist that "Abraham Lincoln has crossed the Rubicon and by one simple act of Justice to the slave links his memory with immortality."[9]

The journalist Thomas Morris Chester gave a speech at the Cooper Institute in New York City three weeks after Lincoln's executive order. The Pennsylvania native called the Emancipation

Proclamation the "grandest" document ever published "beneath the Throne of God."[10] It gave Chester hope that Black people would emerge from slavery to find a more democratic nation awaiting them.

General Rufus Saxton, commander of the Department of the South, told Black Southerners that it was their "duty" to spread the word "loud and clear" that they were free.[11] Some Black leaders were not as optimistic as Saxton. They criticized Lincoln "for doing the very least, rather than the very most, that he could have done against slavery."[12] The proclamation was an example of Lincoln's ability to be pragmatic. The document did not extend liberation to all enslaved people because he recognized the need to keep the loyal border states in the Union.

Before the emancipation declaration, Lincoln had rejected offers to accept Black men in the Union army. In turning down the overture of two Black regiments from Indiana in August 1862, he told the delegation that he had no problem using "all colored men offered as laborers but would not promise to make soldiers of them."[13] A month later, the president reiterated his position on Black enrollment when he informed a religious group from Chicago that he was "not sure" that the military "could do much with the blacks."[14] Lincoln also understood the repercussions that could come if African American troops failed on the battlefield. His critics on all sides would accuse him of "sacrificing black men to spare white ones."[15] With casualties mounting and slow recruitment, it became a military necessity for Lincoln to tap the large reservoir of Black manpower.

Black soldiers knew that it was Lincoln who had given them the opportunity to fight for their country and to prove their patriotism and manhood. The enlistment of Black men into the Union army signaled that the prosecution of the conflict was no longer the responsibility of white men only. Once men of color were allowed to join the fight, courage, not cowardice, defined their performance. By war's end, 180,000 Black men had joined the army and 20,000 had enlisted in the navy.

The establishment of the Bureau of Colored Troops by the War Department a few months after January 1, 1863, signaled the administration's efforts to professionalize the recruitment and organization of African American soldiers. During the years between the proclamation and the end of the war, the tenacious fighting spirit of Black men confirmed that Lincoln had made a wise political and financial investment in them as soldiers. Members of the Black regiments understood that the freedom of their race was tied to the success of the Union army. Major William Eliot Furness of Philadelphia, an officer in the Third USCT, claimed that African Americans "knew, as if by intuition, that their fate hung on the success of the cause; and they waited in patience, and with prayers, ever ready for the day of Jubilee."[16]

There was a sentiment among Black troops that the Emancipation Proclamation also freed whites. After the war, a group of Black veterans reflected on the historical significance of Lincoln's document by noting that it "not only set the colored man free," but it also "set many white men free" as well.[17] Former bondmen also understood the linkage of the proclamation to white people. As the ex-slave Robert R. Grinstead of Oklahoma looked back on slavery, he nuanced his memory with a philosophical bent. He confided, "My viewpoint as to slavery is that it was as much detrimental to the white race as it was to the Negroes, as one elevated ones minds too highly, and the other degraded ones mind too lowly."[18] The humanitarian document helped to ease the conscience of many whites who, like Lincoln, abhorred the concept of some men owning others. Slavery was hurtful to yeomen farmers and poor whites. They could not compete with the free labor system of the North.

Shortly after General Robert E. Lee's surrender, a bullet shortened the life of the beloved leader of African American troops. While the hearts of Black civilians were breaking for the man whom they credited with the emancipation of their race, Black soldiers were mourning the loss of their commander in chief. They expressed their feelings of grief and anger in letters and interviews. Some of the men of the Fifty-Fourth Massachusetts Volunteers, in addition to other Black regiments, diligently preserved their thoughts about the war and the demise of Lincoln. Governor John A. Andrew considered it an honor that the first Black regiment of the North was organized in his state. He said that the regiment would serve as "a means of elevating the people of color hereafter."[19] The troops of the Fifty-Fourth did not disappoint their governor. The regiment could not hide their outrage upon hearing of Lincoln's death. Captain Luis F. Emilio confessed, "There was much bitter feeling indulged in by the soldiery for a time."[20] Colonel Henry N. Hooper, commanding officer of the Fifty-Fourth Massachusetts, indicated that word of Lincoln's death produced hurt and anger among his men. Writing to the adjutant general of Massachusetts, he said, "On the 23rd a cloud settled upon us. Rumors reached us that our President had been foully murdered; we at first could not comprehend it, it was too overwhelming, too lamentable, too distressing. We said quietly 'Now there is *no more* peace, let us turn back, again load our muskets and if necessary exterminate the race that can do such things.' Thus we all felt."[21]

In a letter to the *Christian Recorder*, Private Benjamin M. Bond of Company B of the Fifty-Fourth Massachusetts recalled how their joyful mood turned somber when they realized that Lincoln was dead. Writing from Georgetown, South Carolina, the Maryland native said, "Our emotions of joy and hope are mingled with the deepest sorrow at the loss of our lamented President, who was esteemed by the community at large." Bond's excitement at liberating several thousand in the Palmetto State as part of General Edward E. Potter's raid was tinged with pessimism. His reflection included the view of his fellow soldiers when he asserted that "in spite of the President's Proclamation," these Black people "might have been kept in bondage for many years to come."[22]

The New York native Private Edgar Dinsmore of Company F of the Fifty-Fourth Massachusetts Regiment was in Charleston when John Wilkes Booth killed the president. He reflected on the death of Lincoln in a letter to his fiancée, Carrie Drayton, on May 29, 1865. Dinsmore told his future wife that the death of the Great Emancipator was an "irreparable" loss. He went on to proclaim that African Americans had lost their "Patron Saint and the good of the world a fitting object to emulate." Dinsmore predicted that "Abraham Lincoln will ever be cherished in our hearts, and none will more delight to lisp his name in reverence than the future generations of our people."[23]

One soldier who invoked the names of God and Abraham Lincoln as the two individuals most responsible for their liberation was James C. Taylor, an orderly sergeant of the Ninety-Third United States Colored Infantry. He was certain that it was the Heavenly Father and Lincoln who had purged slavery from the land. "But, God, in his divine wisdom, through the instrumentality of our noble President, Abraham Lincoln," Taylor exclaimed, "saw fit to remove the only dark spot (Slavery) from one of the most glorious flags the sun ever shone upon."[24] The Philadelphian Sergeant John C. Brock of the Forty-Third USCT declared in a letter to the *Christian Recorder* that thousands who once languished in slavery were then "in the ranks of the armies of the Union, hurling avenging justice on those who were the cause of this foul rebellion, and whose sworn purpose was to perpetuate human bondage."[25] Brock was making it clear that Southern politicians and the planter class were guilty of starting the war. It should be noted, however, that soldiers were not the only ones capable of looking at the war in analytical terms.

Kate Drumgoold was a former enslaved person who relocated from Virginia to Brooklyn, New York, after the war. There she fulfilled her dream of becoming a teacher as a way of uplifting her race. She wrote in her autobiography, "[Lincoln has] a green spot in my heart and shall ever keep green while on this side I stay." The Black educator understood that Lincoln's success as commander in chief rested heavily on the shoulders of General Ulysses S. Grant. She praised Grant as "one who will ever be shining bright in the hearts and minds of the whole negro race" and asserted that he "led us to the greatest victory the world has ever known."[26] For Drumgoold, the trinity that delivered African Americans from bondage consisted of God, Lincoln, and Grant. Drumgoold's assessment of Grant's role in the conflict was on point. Once the general assumed his leadership position, the war continued to shift in favor of the Union.

The reactions of the USCT to the death of the Great Emancipator often flowed through the pens of white officers. They routinely described their own states of grief in addition to capturing the sorrow of African American soldiers. Captain Joseph M. Califf of Pennsylvania commanded companies in the Seventh USCT during the last eighteen months of the war. While marching from Burkeville, Virginia, in the direction of Petersburg, they heard about what had happened to Lincoln. In recording the unit's reactions to Booth's fatal attack, the Pennsylvanian wrote, "The news fell upon us like a thunderbolt from a clear sky. Our exultation was turned into mourning. Everyone seemed to feel that it was a personal as well as a national misfortune."[27]

Captain Solon A. Carter of the Eighteenth Army Corps, which also had Black regiments, sent a letter to his wife, Emily, on April 18, 1865, from Raleigh, North Carolina. In documenting the mood of the soldiers headquartered there, Carter stated, "Yesterday the news of the assassination of President Lincoln reached us. What a dreadful thing it is. I think the Country could at this time better afford to lose Grant or Sherman in action or lose a battle, than to lose, Abraham Lincoln."[28] As president and commander in chief of the armed forces, Lincoln's value to the Union army superseded that of his generals.

The white officer Warren Goodale of the 114th United States Colored Infantry reported on the feelings of the regiment about Lincoln in a missive to his children. He said that the troops "were shocked and amazed . . . that our good President Secretary Seward and son had been assassinated at Washington."[29] Because of the confusion that followed the assassination, many in the nation believed that Secretary of State William H. Seward and his son Frederick had suffered the same fate as Lincoln. The news that such reports were inaccurate brought the light of hope to an otherwise dark period. After the war, Carter reflected on the role of the USCT in the emancipation process. He recounted, "The story of the part taken by the colored soldier in the war which resulted in establishing the freedom of his race . . . sprung, at a single bound, from the darkness of servitude to the light of freedom, from a chattel to a man, from a serf to a citizen."[30]

The stand Lincoln had taken against slavery had not waned over time among the freedpeople. The ex-bondman Charles C. Skinner of North Carolina recalled, "With such memories vividly before me, it is any wonder that I feel like worshipping a man like President Lincoln, who brought this condition to an end?"[31] During the war, Lincoln reached the conclusion "that the sin of slavery had to be torn out of the fabric of the union" if freedom were to be meaningful for all Americans.[32] Lincoln knew that slavery was a great injustice that had been perpetrated on a large segment of the African American population by the planters. According to the president, the war, with all its horror, "represented divine retribution" aimed at the whole country for the presence of the infernal institution.[33]

Slavery and Lincoln were on the mind of Lizzie Barnett of Conway, Arkansas, who was originally from Tennessee, during her interview in the 1930s. She recollected a brutal system of "bull whips" and remembered hearing "the awful cries of the slaves." Barnett also connected emancipation to Lincoln's death. She declared, "When de [N-word] war was over and dey didn't fit [fight] any longer, Abe Lincoln sot all de [N-word] free and den got 'sassinated for doin it."[34] Upon reflecting on that tumultuous period, Barnett concluded that the war was about the desperate attempt by planters to maintain their way of life.

There was a direct correlation between the Emancipation Proclamation and the "increased disintegration of slavery."[35] Enslaved people's understanding of the presidential decree was the motivating factor for many of them to leave the plantations in droves. As the U.S. Army moved through the Southern states, they attached themselves to the men in blue. A common sight during the Civil War were contraband camps established by the Union army that housed Black refugees. The term *contraband* was first used by Benjamin F. Butler while he was stationed at Fort Monroe, Virginia, in 1861. The Union general refused to return to their owner a few escaped men who sought refuge in his camp. As the war progressed

A group of refugees consisting of men, women, and children in Cumberland Landing, Virginia in 1862. Contraband camps such as this one were symbols of freedom, hardship, and mourning after the assassination. LC-DIG-cwpb-01005, Prints and Photographs Division, Library of Congress.

and Union victories mounted, those in bondage became even more defiant in their push for freedom. The upheaval of the war had created a state of disorder in their world. But the conflict also provided them with the opportunity to break their chains. By the thousands, Blacks strove to eke out an existence in conditions that were far from ideal. Inadequate food and shelter, poor sanitation, and overcrowding contributed to sickness coursing through the camps. The life of the freedmen was made even more challenging because of the inconsistency in the administration of the camps. Disputes between civil authorities and army officials often left the former captives in a state of confusion. Added to the humanitarian crisis was grief when Lincoln took his last breath inside the Petersen House. The refugees joined with other Americans in mourning the president's tragic end.[36]

The refugee camp known as Freedmen's Village, which was located at General Robert E. Lee's former estate in Arlington, was an exception to the misery found at other places.[37] The Virginia camp distinguished itself from other sites across the South because of its competent officials, medical facility, school, and opportunities for men and women to learn trades. When word of the assassination reached the village, the abolitionist and activist Sojourner Truth organized a memorial service for the slain leader. Truth believed that Lincoln's reward for the destruction of slavery was a seat in the Kingdom of Heaven.[38]

George A. Huron of Indiana was headquartered at City Point, Virginia, when the bloodletting came to an end. Huron remembered that "a sound of lamentation" at the refugee camp was an indication that something horrific had occurred. He wrote, "The voice of sorrow came from [the] direction of the negro camp. . . . Thousands of negroes were wringing their hands and in indescribable wailing were giving expression to their great grief. I met a grayheaded old man. The intensity of his anguish cannot be pictured in words. I enquired the cause of his sorrow, and was struck dumb by his answer." With "tears streaming down his cheeks," the man told Huron, "President Lincoln is dead, he's been murdered." Huron added that the assassination of the nation's chief was a crushing loss for Black Americans.[39] The demonstrative outpouring of sorrow by numerous people previously held in bondage was doubtless an unforgettable sight. Grief circulated through the camp as if it were carried by the wind.

After the assassination, there was a tendency for Americans to compare Lincoln to George Washington. In actuality, the comparison had its origin in Lincoln's last speech in Springfield. The president-elect told the crowd of admirers who had gathered at the depot in his hometown to say goodbye that he was embarking on an endeavor that was "greater than that which rested upon Washington."[40] By connecting himself to Washington, Lincoln had set the stage for the first and sixteenth presidents to be connected in American memory. The death of Washington in December 1799 produced mourning throughout the country as Americans paused to honor the nation's first president. Washington led the country during its infant years, and Lincoln preserved the republic that he had helped to create. The "people admired Washington," claims one scholar, "but they loved as well as admired Lincoln."[41] The ownership of enslaved people by Washington diminished his reputation in the eyes of people of color. His will called for their release at Mount Vernon upon the death of his wife. Citizens of color based their preference for Lincoln on the role he played in their emancipation. The Presbyterian preacher Reverend Joseph Prime believed that African Americans' selection of Lincoln over Washington was appropriate. He said, "If the American people have reason to rejoice in the life and labors of a Washington, then the colored people of our country have a much greater reason to rejoice that Abraham Lincoln was permitted to occupy the executive chair, as Chief Ruler of this nation."[42]

As the month of April was coming to an end, information about the murder drifted to Vicksburg. The *New York Tribune* noted that "the assassination of President Lincoln fell with grievous force upon the Blacks in the rebellious States." In Vicksburg a reporter for the *Tribune* captured "one of the most touching spectacles" that he had ever seen. He wrote, "The colored people, however, are the most demonstrative. A portrait of Mr. Lincoln was placed in front of a store, and has been continually surrounded by a crowd of them, each sorrowful, and many gazing with tearful eyes upon the shadow of him to whom their entire race had somehow learned to look upon as their redeemer, leading them out of the gloom of bondage into the light of liberty."[43]

Two days after Lincoln's death, Black residents of Albany, New York, assembled at the Hamilton Street African Methodist Episcopal Church, under the leadership of William H. Anthony. One of the resolutions drafted by them proclaimed that Lincoln had been the guiding force "in striking off the chains from so many millions of our brethren" and that his name would be remembered by African Americans "for generations to come."[44] The Colored Union League Club of Connecticut, a patriotic organization, held a meeting at the African Methodist Episcopal Zion Church in Bridgeport in April 1865 to memorialize the president. The members credited him with extending freedom "throughout the United States."[45]

In mid-September 1865, the Colored Men's Convention of the State of Michigan assembled at the Second Baptist Church in Detroit. Toward the end of the proceedings, the convention issued a resolution in honor of the president framed against the backdrop of the Emancipation Proclamation. The statement praised Lincoln for marching "to the prison house" and unlocking the gate to allow "the poor slave" to walk out.[46]

Several hundred African Americans attended a speech by Major Martin R. Delany on Saint Helena Island in South Carolina after the war. He fully intended for his words to reverberate around the country. He was unequivocal in his oration about the role the USCT had played in the outcome of the military struggle. The major roared, "I want to tell you one thing, do you know that if it was not for the black man this war never would have been brought to a close with success to the Union, and the liberty of your race if it had not been for the negro?"[47] In praising Black people, Delany did not tell the whole story. Other individuals and institutions had a hand in helping to remove slavery from its entrenched position in the Southern states. In addition to officers and enlisted men, "legislatures, judges, and generals played crucial roles in ending slavery, as did enslaved people, who seized freedom at every opportunity."[48] In the final analysis, many hands were working simultaneously toward the same goal of liberation for America's enslaved men, women, and children.

The teacher Elizabeth Hyde Botume of the New England Freedmen's Aid Society was at Hilton Head when word of Robert E. Lee's surrender and news of the assassination reached there. According to the Bostonian, the formerly enslaved "were wild with delight over" the collapse of the Confederacy, and "they worked all day, and sang and shouted all night." A week later, "the joy of the final victory" was replaced by sorrow. Botume recorded that "some of the young men came together for a little singing and shouting, but the older people looked very grave." Botume recalled an African American woman who approached her begging "for a leetle bit o'black to pit aroun' the tail o' my coat [gown] to mourn for poor Papa Sam."[49] As the nation prepared to say goodbye to the president in the District of Columbia, the freedmen on Hilton Head turned their attention to conducting a funeral for Lincoln in a schoolhouse. The Boston educator remembered the prayer of one of the leaders of the service, who "called the martyred president by every tender and endearing tone of which he could think." He ended his supplication with the refrain, "Massa Linkum! our 'dored Redeemer an' Saviour an' Frien'! Amen!"[50]

As the war ended, it was obvious that Booth's attempt to invalidate the work of the U.S. Army by killing the president had failed. The Union had been preserved, and white Southerners did not resurrect the Confederacy. Indeed, the abolition of slavery constituted the heaviest blow to the planter class. As a champion of the Thirteenth Amendment, Lincoln was preparing the nation for the burial of the egregious institution of slavery.

Black clerics were adept at convincing enslaved people that they might one day see Lincoln for themselves. Some people of color were thinking about a heavenly reunion with Lincoln before his death in 1865. This was the case two years earlier. The Baptist Church of Christ of Beaufort, South Carolina, adopted a resolution expressing the hope of one day fellowshipping with Lincoln in the world beyond the grave. "We never expect to meet your face on earth," the statement declared, "but may we meet in a better world than this;—this is our humble prayer."[51] Many African Americans believed that when their time on earth was over, a reunion in Paradise of the emancipator and the emancipated was a real possibility. Although people of color were weighted down with sorrow, they could find solace in the fact that the death of slavery had preceded the death of Lincoln. Formerly enslaved people were grateful to God for sending them a deliverer whom they believed was mingling in the Heavenly Kingdom with the saints.

CHAPTER FOUR

Their Earthly Moses

THE ANALOGIES BETWEEN Abraham Lincoln and Moses, the leader and lawgiver of the Israelites, did not escape the attention of the enslaved race. In their quest for freedom, they found inspiration for the journey to the land of liberation in the Old Testament book of Exodus, where God delivers the chosen people from centuries of Egyptian bondage under the leadership of Moses. By using the story of the Exodus as their theological guide, enslaved men and women substituted Lincoln for Moses and themselves for the Israelites. As Black people emerged from the inhumane institution, they associated Lincoln with the virtues of Christ. According to John E. Washington, the bondmen worshiped Lincoln as if he were "an earthly incarnation of the Savior of mankind."[1] Lincoln's faith was well known among his family, friends, and inner circle. In no small way, the president's apotheosis had to do with his connection to and identification with religious symbols. Lincoln frequently acknowledged his reliance on and guidance from God.

Many Black people believed that the Almighty had placed him in power for the purpose of leading the country at a pivotal moment in its history. An editorial appearing in the *Christian Recorder* at the time of the assassination pointed out that Lincoln "had led this nation through its bleak night of trouble.... Like Moses of old, he reached the mountain's brow, and viewed the glory that was promised to his people. But as he was preparing for the last great step, he fell—a Martyr to his cause, and a Sacrifice to his country."[2]

For multitudes in the Black community, it was God's intention that slavery would not remain a permanent institution in the nation.

African Americans credited Lincoln, their earthly Moses, with seizing the opportunity presented by the internal strife to strike a powerful blow against the planters' system of forced labor. Enslaved Americans believed that God responded to their prayers by causing a great civil war to fall upon the land. In 1861, the famous abolitionist Harriet Tubman theorized that the Civil War was the catalyst for freedom for those in bondage. She was affectionately known as the Moses of the Underground Railroad. Tubman suggested that freedom for enslaved people would result in victory for the Union. Tubman said, "God won't let Massa Linkum beat the South till he do de right ting. Massa Linkum he great man, and I'se poor [N-word]; but dis [N-word] can tell Massa Linkum how to save money and de young men. He do it by setting de [N-word] free."[3] To the downtrodden and oppressed bondmen, Lincoln was their last best hope on earth.

Black captives were acutely aware that Southern aristocrats were losing their grip on slavery as the war progressed. A soldier of the Fourteenth United States Colored Troops (USCT) from Tennessee told the president that "thousands in the army rejoice in your work and pray for you that you may be sustained till the great work which God has called you to is fully accomplished."[4] Northern ministers routinely preached that Southern states played a significant part in bringing on the war and should be punished for their transgression.[5] In 1863, a white soldier stated that slavery "was the cause of so much bloodshed and suffering" and that it was "heinous in the sight of God."[6] The Black Oberlin, Ohio, resident Carrie V. Still was also dismayed by the carnage of the war. Writing in 1864 to her friend Jacob C. White Jr., an educator and Philadelphian, she opined that "God caused a heavy judgement to fall" upon the nation because of its failure to repent for the sin of slavery.[7]

As Americans prepared to go to church on Easter Sunday, the president of the United States lay in repose in the White House. Ministers across the land discarded their prepared Easter sermons and quickly substituted them with exhortations honoring the slain leader. An inseparable "dimension of the mourning rituals" was the eulogy, which helped to soothe those who were grief-stricken.[8] These were poignant expressions that extolled the personal qualities and, in some cases, the historical significance of the deceased. The extraordinary number of panegyric statements about Lincoln made it clear that he was the leading disciple of the gospel of American exceptionalism.

The Sunday morning following the assassination, worshipers heard Black preachers connect Lincoln to Moses. On Easter morning, Reverend Jacob Thomas of the African Methodist Episcopal Zion Church in Troy, New York, told his congregation that, "to us as a despised people," Lincoln "was a second Moses—a second Daniel in wisdom." The parson brought his sermon to a close by telling the mourners that the Heavenly Father had selected Lincoln "for a special purpose, and that having accomplished the labor assigned him, he has gone to his rest."[9] The grief-stricken flock at Reverend Joseph A. Prime's church, Liberty Street Presbyterian, heard him say on Easter Sunday that the "cruel system" of bondage had degraded and enslaved both Black and white Southerners. According to the pastor, "God sent forth the modern Moses to deliver this people from the curse" of slavery.[10] On the day of Lincoln's funeral in Washington, a large crowd met at the Zion Baptist Church in Cincinnati on Third Street to pay homage to the martyred president. Reverend Wallace Shelton told the congregants that on the morning of the president's death, "there was gathering gloom in the heavens and in the hearts of men, and weeping in the clouds and the eyes of the people." The "Moses of his people," Reverend Shelton claimed, had carried out God's plan.[11]

African American ministers were skilled at portraying Lincoln as the pilot who directed the flight of deliverance for those in bondage. After the conflict, Reverend Simeon Beard told formerly enslaved people that "God intended, through this war, that, like the Red Sea, while the nation rendered itself asunder, you should pass through free."[12] The South Carolina native Reverend James Lynch of the African Methodist Episcopal Church preached that "the freedmen of the South" routinely held "for Mr. Lincoln a reverence next to that felt for the blessed Saviour." The Methodist cleric noted that the president had led the captives "through the red sea of blood to freedom" and that if the liberty of Black Americans were ever endangered, "the blood of Abraham Lincoln will speak."[13]

Lizzie Hart of Ohio lamented with fellow mourners in an article she penned for the *Christian Recorder* that Lincoln had survived the war but was denied the chance to accomplish the restoration of the nation. Hart observed that he "lived, through, the great struggle for American liberty—to see the dawn of peace; but just as he was about to realize the fruition of his hopes and labors, he was brutally" murdered. Hart claimed that no death in American history had produced such widespread grief. "There never was a time since the birth of the country," she said, "when such universal sadness prevailed."[14] Lincoln was on the mind of the residents of Xenia, Ohio, home to Wilberforce University, the oldest private Black college in the nation. When the news reached Xenia, the streets filled with mourners lamenting the loss of their "Moses," whom they remembered as "great and noble."[15]

Days after the assassination, a letter from Jane Swisshelm appeared in a Minnesota newspaper in which she described the reaction of Blacks in Washington to the crime. According to her, "The presence of the thousands of Freed-people who regarded Abraham Lincoln as their Moses, adds to the impressiveness of the scene." People of color, Swisshelm recorded, wailed "with a feeling akin to despair." Swisshelm concluded her account with the observation that many African Americans went without food to purchase a piece of black cloth with which to adorn their abodes.[16]

Numerous Black soldiers let it be known that God occupied a central place in their lives. Like many Americans after the assassination, soldiers of the USCT sought comfort in religious services. Both officers and enlisted men wept during an Easter service at Camp William Penn, just north of Philadelphia. The minister told the men that the day was fast approaching when their pain and anguish would cease to exist. The cleric said, "You must endeavor to do your duty! God, for some wise purpose, has allowed him to be slain! But, the day is not far distant when there will be a Moses raised up to conduct you through the sea of sorrow which now surrounds you."[17] This was the parson's way of telling the Black troops that God would not forsake them.

Sergeant Elijah P. Marrs of the Twelfth Colored Heavy Artillery recorded in his memoir the response of his regiment upon hearing the account. They were in Bowling Green, Kentucky, as the war ended. The sergeant recollected that the men of the unit wept upon learning of the event. Against the backdrop of the assassination, he also confessed that their "Moses" was gone.[18] Another soldier, Sergeant John C. Brock of the Forty-Third USCT, referred to the president as "the fearless patriot, the wise statesman . . . who has guided the ship of state safely through the storm of four long years of unparalleled war, turmoil and bloodshed." Brock announced that he was pleased that God had allowed Lincoln "to see the fruits of his toil" before the loss of his life.[19] An officer in a Black regiment placed Lincoln in company with the leader of the Israelites in a letter to his wife. Writing to her in 1863, several months after the presidential decree of freedom, he said, "I begin to look upon him some as the ancient Jews did upon Moses—as a chosen instrument of God for the deliverance of the Nation."[20]

The ex-slave Frank Hughes was certain that their liberation had been ordained by a higher authority. He told an interviewer in the 1930s what he thought about the president. "I thinks about him jes like I did about Moses. I think it was de will of de lawd to talk to Abraham Lincoln through de spirit, to work out a plan to set" the bondmen free.[21] Reflecting on the assassination, Elizabeth Keckley asserted that "the Moses of my people had fallen in the hour of his triumph. . . . Fame had woven her choicest chaplet for his brow. Though the brow was cold and pale in death, the chaplet should not fade, for God had studded it with the glory of the eternal stars."[22] Blacks were not ashamed of their exuberant reverence for the president. Lincoln's faith and the manner of his death were contributing factors in Black Americans' glorification of him.

The adoration of emancipated people for Lincoln was much like Christians' devotion to their Creator. African Americans overwhelmingly identified themselves as Christians. By comparing

Lincoln to Jesus Christ, Blacks summarily elevated him to godlike status. Lewis Jenkins, who spent years in bondage, doubtless expressed the thought of many freedpeople when he declared that Lincoln was a benevolent and humble servant of God. Jenkins concluded that the president "died helpin' the poor" people of his race.[23] The former bondman Robert Burns declared, "We all thought Abraham Lincoln was our God."[24] An editorial appearing in a Black newspaper headquartered in San Francisco told its readers that the slain leader was "but one degree inferior" to the Son of God.[25] Rarely did ex-bondmen blame the Holy Savior for their condition of servitude. And seldom did the late president supersede the Almighty God as the principal agent of their freedom. To Black Southerners, Lincoln represented an expectation of a better life for them.

Black Americans realized that one of the striking similarities between Moses and Lincoln was that neither of them reached the Promised Land with those whom they had led out of bondage. Nonetheless, both martyrs had completed the tasks assigned to them by God. Despite the chaos and perplexity caused by Lincoln's death, Black Christians were not in the habit of questioning God's authority. This view was articulated by the journalist and nationalist Martin R. Delany, who was one of the most distinguished Black leaders of the antebellum period. Lincoln commissioned the Harvard-trained physician as a major in the 104th USCT two months before the curtain closed on the Confederacy. A few days after the evacuation of Charleston, Delany had the privileged of meeting with the president at the White House. Delany had gone to Lincoln's home in February 1865 to present him with a proposal for the creation of a Black army. The physician turned soldier doubtless had impressed Lincoln, who called him "an extraordinary and intelligent black man."[26] With the Confederate States on life support, Delany's proposition became obsolete. To help Black mourners deal with their hurt, he urged them to accept the removal of Lincoln from the presidential office as the will of the Supreme Being. "God in his inscrutable providence, has suffered this," he proclaimed, "and we bow with meek and humble resignation to his Divine will, because He does all things well."[27]

Martin R. Delany (1812–85), Black nationalist, abolitionist, and recruiter, was commissioned as a major in February 1865, making him the highest-ranking African American field officer in the Union army during the war. Courtesy of the National Portrait Gallery, Smithsonian Institution.

While in New Berne, North Carolina, Mary Ann Starkey, president of the Colored Women's Relief Association, wrote to her abolitionist friend Edward W. Kinsley of Massachusetts. She told him that African Americans found a measure of comfort in the belief that the Divine Creator had removed Lincoln once his work on earth had been finished. She affirmed, "Had I written you a few days ago I should have rejoiced over the *glorious* news, now there is little heart left for rejoicing since the sad news of the death of our President. It must be alright, as God permitted it, but it does seem very hard to us—were it not for the thought that there was one over our nation whom death nor disease can never affect, discouragement would indeed fill our hearts."[28] The *Columbus Gazette* also claimed that the assassination had been sanctioned by the Omnipotent One. "The hand of God is in this affliction, and the very death of our lamented Chief Magistrate," the newspaper editorialized on April 21, 1865, "may be the means of bringing about the salvation of the nation."[29] The Troy minister Reverend Jacob Thomas reminded his flock, "An all-wise God has permitted this great grief to come upon us. Let us look to him for deliverance in the time of our distress. We are humbled, we are mortified, we are brought very low." He called on African Americans to remember that Lincoln was then in heaven "mingling with those kindred spirits who went before him."[30]

African American churches were at the forefront of extolling the virtues and Christlike qualities associated with Lincoln in the weeks and months following his death. Black preachers encouraged their charges to honor him by emulating his best qualities and asserted that in so doing they would be embracing the teachings of Christ. In commemorating the slain leader, Black religious institutions frequently illuminated Lincoln's virtues of humility, integrity, forgiveness, simplicity, and faith, which resonated with people of color. African Americans also identified with Lincoln because of his impoverished background, his lack of education, and the unfortunate events that brought sorrow to his life. The assassination's occurring on Good Friday was not lost on most African

Americans. They knew that the death of Jesus Christ had also occurred on Good Friday. Blacks believed that both men had died for
a higher purpose. To them, Lincoln had died to save the nation
from slavery and Jesus had died to save humanity from sin.

Reverend Shelton made it plain that Lincoln's Christlike characteristics were among his outstanding human qualities. He placed
the president in exalted company when he posited that Jesus's
"mercy and truth are personified in ABRAHAM LINCOLN."[31] In
New Orleans, Reverend George W. Le Vere offered a eulogy for the
martyred leader in May 1865. Le Vere had met Lincoln in November 1863, and a few months later Lincoln appointed him as chaplain
of the Twentieth United States Colored Infantry. In the estimation of the eulogist, Lincoln was concerned not about wealth or
recognition but rather about the welfare of the nation. Chaplain
Le Vere concluded by calling on African Americans to write Lincoln's name in their family Bibles as a way of honoring the "great
and good man."[32] Since it was a common practice for Bibles to be
handed down, such a notation would make it unlikely that his
name would be forgotten by future generations of Black people.

Private Isaac J. Hill of Pennsylvania joined the Twenty-Ninth
Connecticut Colored troops in the winter of 1863. In his brief history of the unit after the war, the private recollected that Lincoln
"was meek, like the Lord and Savior, and forgave his enemies to the
last. I fancy I can almost hear him say in his dying moments, 'Father,
forgive them for they know not what they do.'"[33] Hill was convinced that Lincoln would have wanted Black Americans to forgive
his assassin like Jesus Christ forgave those who crucified him.

Years after the war, Sergeant Charles S. Tatten, also of the
Twenty-Ninth Connecticut Colored, remembered Lincoln as an
individual who possessed virtues in abundance. The Hartford native claimed that the president "was absolutely honest, not only to
others but to himself." Furthermore, the Black veteran declared
that Lincoln "was homely, a man of brains, yet modest and humble,
a kindly man, a Christian, a wise man, and *brave*."[34] Reverend Jacob
Thomas enthused that "one of the most prominent features in the

character of our departed friend was his merciful disposition even toward his foes."[35] An officer commanding the USCT in the Department of Tennessee surveyed the response of his soldiers to the demise of the president. He made it known that the men regarded Lincoln with a "pure and genuine affection . . . never before entertained for any man by so large a number."[36]

Many African Americans had so much deep-hearted admiration for Lincoln that they felt as though they had a personal relationship with him. An editorial in the *Christian Recorder* a few days after the assassination spoke about Lincoln in lofty terms. The newspaper claimed that he "was the true embodiment of the good and noble qualities which go toward making a perfect American citizen." The editor concluded that Lincoln was not only "honest to a fault" but also kind-hearted.[37]

The editor of a Black journal stated that Lincoln's altruistic "tendencies were as natural to his heart as the bubbling water from a spring."[38] Annie L. Burton, who grew up in bondage on a plantation in Alabama, commented on the president's virtue. She remembered that despite Lincoln's "ungainly figure, ill-fitting clothes, the soul of the man had conquered even the stubborn South, while the cold-blooded North was stricken to the heart. The noblest one of all had been taken."[39] Lincoln's inner convictions rather than his outward appearance served him well as president.

More than any other Black leader, Frederick Douglass knew that Lincoln's Christian character was one of his distinguishing features. On the afternoon of Lincoln's death, he joined others at city hall in Rochester for a memorial service. In Rochester as in numerous communities across the North and the South, people of color witnessed "a springtime of relief turned overnight into horror and mourning."[40] Because he was not formally invited, Douglass's remarks were straight from the heart. He told the listeners that the death of Lincoln was "a personal as well as national calamity." Like many of his fellow African Americans, the prolific speaker "imagined Lincoln as a Christ-like martyr whose death promised" to generate a new sense of freedom in the nation.[41]

Among some African Americans, a notion persisted that Lincoln possessed supernatural or Christlike powers. A group of Black men working on the wharf in Beaufort, South Carolina, during the war were discussing what the president meant to their race "when an aged, white headed negro, a 'praise man' (as the phrase is) amongst them, with all the solemnity and earnestness of an old prophet broke forth: What do you know 'bout Massa Linkum? Massa Linkum be ebrewhere. He walk de earth like de Lord."[42] The educator Laura M. Towne heard a comment bordering on supernaturalism when an ex-slave told her that "Lincoln died for we, Christ died for we, and me believe him de same mans."[43]

The brightest star in the American political galaxy went dark when the deadly conspiracy of a fanatical actor succeeded. Major Delany called the event a tragic affair that "brought our country to mourning by the untimely death of the humane, the benevolent, the philanthropic, the generous, the beloved, the able, the wise, the great, and good man, the President of the United States, Abraham Lincoln, the Just."[44] Delany's inspirational message was designed to encourage Americans to be more Lincolnesque in their interactions with each other. The Black major was inviting Americans to use the president's life as a model by which to live.

The New Orleans newspaper the *Black Republican* maintained that African Americans and Lincoln were inseparable and that the president was worthy of their reverence of him. The editor told its readers, "Hereafter, through all time, wherever the Black Race may be known in the world: whenever and wherever it shall lay the foundations of its power: build its cities and rear its temples. It will sacredly preserve if not deify the name *of Abraham, the Martyr.*"[45]

With the assassination fresh in the minds of Black Americans, they could only hope that Lincoln would be succeeded by a modern Joshua who would complete the journey to the Promised Land. For many decades after the war, Black people continued to struggle for social, political, and economic justice. Their standing in American life received a significant boost when God sent them a modern-day Moses in the person of Reverend Martin Luther King Jr. But like Lincoln and Moses before him, King would not reach the Promised

Land. The land of Paradise is still out of reach for many Americans who are impoverished, downtrodden, oppressed, and bewildered. Those who had been stripped of their human dignity by bondage for so many decades saw in Lincoln a man who was protective, inspirational, and supportive.

CHAPTER FIVE

Father, Friend, and Benefactor

I T WAS NOT UNCOMMON FOR African Americans to refer to Abraham Lincoln as their father, friend, and benefactor. They believed that, like a trusted family member, he was the person whom they could appeal to for help and depend on when adversity came their way. Furthermore, they sometimes petitioned the president by writing to him. Lincoln greeted and treated Black people with dignity and respect in both Springfield and Washington. His ubiquitous nature helps to explain Black Americans' attachment to him. Some of them had read his speeches, and others had heard Black leaders speak about him. Lincoln himself noted the importance of "fathers" in his famous Gettysburg Address when he said, "Our fathers brought forth on this continent, a new nation, conceived in Liberty, and dedicated to the proposition that all men are created equal."[1]

African Americans frequently thought of Lincoln as "Father Abraham" before and after his death. To them, he represented such a person because he occupied the preeminent position in the federal government. It was commonplace for Americans during the nineteenth century to "imagine governmental authority as parental."[2] They were convinced that, as the nation's authoritative leader, Lincoln took an interest in their well-being as if he were their father. With authority came responsibility. For most of America's history, the father was the person who provided for and protected the family.

For former enslaved people, Lincoln's assassination was synonymous with losing a family member. Frederick Douglass gave voice to this point when he responded to Mary Lincoln, who had sent him a gift associated with the president. On August 17, 1865, he sent a letter to Mary in which he said, "I certainly do thank you most sincerely for your thoughtful kindness in making me the owner of a cane which was formerly the property and the favorite walking stick of your lamented husband, the honored and venerated president of the United States." Douglass concluded his correspondence by assuring the widowed First Lady that the memento not only would remain "sacred" to him but would also serve "as an indication of [Lincoln's] human interest in the welfare of [Douglass's] whole race."[3]

The emotional attachment of many Black and white Americans to the man from Illinois was inescapable. A letter from a Black mourner in Cincinnati to Robert Hamilton, editor of the *Weekly Anglo-African*, told people of color that Lincoln's death was tantamount to the race suffering the loss of its father. He referenced "the nation's bereavement, viz—the untimely end of our great and good President Lincoln—Father Abraham, for such he has been indeed to our race."[4] A Black woman in North Carolina was so despondent upon hearing the news that "she felt as if both her father and mother had died at the same time."[5] A few days after the assassination, the Colored Union League Club of Bridgeport served as a forum for Black people of that city to express their "feelings on the loss of a friend and Father of this country, Abraham Lincoln."[6]

Some people of color remembered that Lincoln's assassination coincided with unforgettable events in their own lives. They recalled where they were and what they were doing when the sad announcement reached them. An African American widow, Caroline Lewis, was living in Louisville when the war came to an end. According to Lewis, "she was big with child" when Lincoln's life was taken by an assassin. She recollected that she was going up the stairs when a neighbor rushed in to let her know "that father Lincoln had been shot." The horrendous news jolted her. Because of Lewis's condition, the neighbor cautioned her not "to give way to excitement." She gave birth to a girl shortly after Lincoln's passing.[7]

The death of Lincoln represented a loss not only for African Americans but for the country as well. This point was made by Reverend Wallace Shelton in a sermon honoring the president. He announced that both the nation and his people had lost their father. The Cincinnati minister declared that had Lincoln's "assassins given us the choice, to deliver him or ourselves to death, we would have said, take me; take father, take mother, sister, brother; but do not take the life of the father of this people. But this privilege was not granted us."[8] In New Berne, North Carolina, the Black preacher Reverend Isaac Felton delivered a sermon in which he assured the listeners that "when the light in the East was discernible and the day about breaking, God took Father Abraham up."[9] In 1864, Reverend Felton had been part of a Black delegation from North Carolina that visited Lincoln at his home on Pennsylvania Avenue to appeal for suffrage.

Charleston, the leading port city in South Carolina, was one city where anger, joy, and sorrow occupied the same space simultaneously. It was not lost on the Black people of Charleston that it was through their city that tens of thousands of their ancestors had entered the United States in chains. The city was liberated by their descendants. Word of the collapse of the historic place known as the "cradle of secession" quickly spread throughout the Union army. Three days after the federal takeover, Lieutenant Colonel Albert Rogall, commander of the 118th United States Colored Troops (USCT) stationed near Richmond, wrote in his diary, "Good news that Charleston is in our possession."[10]

The sight of Black men in blue uniforms produced hatred among some white civilians of the captured city. To them, it was an aberration that former enslaved people had joined the Union army. The jubilation that accompanied the fall of Charleston in mid-February 1865 was replaced with despair two months later. Lieutenant Colonel Charles B. Fox, commanding officer of the Fifty-Fifth Massachusetts, recalled that "scarcely a colored person could be met in the streets" of the city who was not laden with sorrow.[11] The correspondent for the *New York Tribune* in Charleston encapsulated the agony that had fallen upon people of color there through the lens of a lamenter. The reporter wrote that one mourner's "heart told her that he whom Heaven had sent in answer to her prayers was lying in a bloody grave, and she and her race were left *father-less*."[12] A Black woman in Charleston offered a bit of advice to her community that was burdened with so much pain. She moaned, "Pears like we all ought to put on black for him for he was a mighty good father to us."[13]

The Fifth USCT, one of two Black regiments raised in Ohio, was present at the surrender of Joseph E. Johnston to William T. Sherman in North Carolina. While there, the "regiment received the sad tidings of the death of President Lincoln, when men of iron nerves" wept like children who had lost their father.[14] African American troops knew that Lincoln was the architect of the Black regiments, which was one of the greatest accomplishments of his presidency. Captain Charles Griswold of Company B of the Twenty-Ninth Connecticut Colored Regiment was in Maryland when John Wilkes Booth made good on his promise. Griswold saw a similarity between children losing their father and men in blue losing their commander in chief. He told a family member that "no one loved Abraham Lincoln better than his soldiers," who "respected him and mourned at his death."[15] An officer of Black troops doubtless captured the sentiment of his men when he told his wife, "I am getting to regard Old Abe almost as a *Father*—to almost venerate him—so earnestly do I believe in his earnestness, fidelity, honesty, & Patriotism."[16]

When Richmond fell to the Union army, Black soldiers were the first to enter the evacuated city. The president visited to get a first-hand look at those whom he had lifted from bondage. They received Lincoln as if he were their father coming home to check on them. The *Christian Recorder* published a missive under the title "Letter from Richmond" on April 22, 1865, written by the ex-bondman and chaplain of the Twenty-Eighth United States Colored Infantry Garland H. White. Chaplain White captured the response of Black Richmonders to Lincoln's visit when he wrote, "I never saw so many colored people in all my life, women and children of all sizes running after father or master Abraham, as they called him. To see the colored people, one would think they had all gone crazy."[17] In the estimation of Michael Burlingame, "Few things contributed more to Lincoln's success as president than his ability to inspire the kind of confidence that children accord to a benevolent father."[18]

A lieutenant of a Black regiment commented on the loss in a letter to his sister. He wrote, "With us of the U.S. Colored Army the death of Lincoln is indeed the loss of a friend. From him we received our commission—and toward him we have even looked as toward a Father."[19] When word of what had taken place at Ford's Theatre spread to Texas, the African American sailor Jack Halliards, serving aboard the U.S. gunboat *Kennebec* near Galveston, ruminated on the crime that had occurred more than 1,400 miles away. The Black sailor made a point of linking the deceased president to the country and to African Americans. He affirmed that "the nation cannot but feel or realize that we have lost in his sudden demise, a father of his country, a true and tried friend of the downtrodden and oppressed, and a Christian soldier of God's grace."[20]

As Booth moved through the countryside to evade apprehension, General Winfield S. Hancock, commanding general of the Middle Military Division, issued an appeal to Black citizens of Washington, Maryland, and Virginia to help capture Lincoln's killer. At the end of his appeal, the general was hopeful that African Americans would remain vigilant in their search for the gunman. Hancock also tapped into African Americans' emotional connection to Lincoln as a friend and father figure. He told them, "But I feel that you need no such stimulus [reward money] as this. You will hunt down this cowardly assassin of your best friend as you would the murderer of your own father. Do this, and God, whose servant has been slain, and the country which has given you freedom, will bless you for this noble act of duty."[21] Since federal soldiers including Black troops were searching for Booth, this was another way in which men of color contributed to the military.

Black people mourned for Lincoln as a friend whom they had known for many years. On the day of the funeral in Washington,

D.C., the *New York Times* printed an editorial that claimed that the president "was a kind of prophet and divine leader" to Black Southerners. The statement noted that "he was known to be their great friend, and was looked forward to as their deliverer."[22] Two weeks after the assassination, the *Weekly Anglo-African* published a letter from a Virginia mourner who said, "To none is this so great a shock as to the freedmen, of the South. . . . They are completely thunder stricken and humiliated, they have lost, they suppose, their last great friend, and seem partly in despair."[23]

This was also the case for the men of the Black regiments who fought with dogged determination so as not to disappoint their "friend" the commander in chief. Sergeant Charles H. Davis of Pennsylvania and the 108th USCT acknowledged the connection between freedom and Lincoln when he claimed that the president's fall brought pain to Black people. He maintained that Lincoln "was the oppressed Americans' friend, who cherish his name as a household word." Davis concluded that of all Black Americans, formerly enslaved people, "for whom he spoke the word of freedom," were the greatest mourners.[24]

Julia Wilbur, a white abolitionist and suffragist from New York, visited the Black army hospital L'Ouverture Hospital in Alexandria, Virginia, days after the horrendous event. Wilbur's observation of the Black soldiers recovering from wounds led her to concede that they were certain that they had "lost a friend."[25] The assassination was on the minds of attendees at a convention of Black soldiers when they drafted a resolution in memory of Lincoln. The delegates wrote that it was "*Resolved*, That we mourn, as we ever must, the sad fate of the martyr-President, Abraham Lincoln, the great Emancipator, and devoted friend of our race."[26]

Not far from Charleston, the Twenty-Sixth USCT was stationed at Fort Duane, near Beaufort, when the light went out on the slaveholders' rebellion. On May 20, an African American periodical printed a letter from Private George Duval in which he revealed that his regiment was both sorrowful and angry. He told the editor, "I will endeavor to pen you a few lines in regard to the feelings of the soldiers in the 26th Regt., about our good friend, President Abraham Lincoln. We all mourn the loss of him." Duval then added, "We all swore we would have revenge for our President."[27] There is no evidence that the troops of the Twenty-Sixth engaged in any retribution against Confederate soldiers or white Southerners. However, the scene was different in Charleston when Union forces occupied the city. Some soldiers of the federal army, in addition to criminal elements of the city, exacted a measure of revenge on white residents by pillaging and destroying property.

The adoption of the chief executive as a friend of people of color could be heard emanating from Black churches. Reverend Jacob Thomas ended his Easter eulogy by telling the members that Lincoln had been "our true friend and we never can forget him."[28] The Troy preacher Reverend Joseph A. Prime told his charges that their expression of sorrow was justified. He bellowed, "None feel that they have lost so true and tried a friend as the millions of bond and freed men of the south."[29] The personal response of a Black woman at Fortress Monroe, Virginia, was obviously instructed by the Holy Scriptures. She acknowledged that Lincoln was human and God was immortal. "They killed our best friend," she declared. "But God be living yet. They can't kill Him."[30]

Black editors were among the influential voices spreading the word that Lincoln was a friend to the downtrodden and destitute. An editorial in the *Weekly Anglo-African* called on African Americans to cherish the memory of Lincoln, who "was the friend of the bondman, and died a martyr to liberty."[31] The *Black Republican* of New Orleans was unequivocal in its declaration that the death of Lincoln was a stunning blow to people of color. Reverend Stephen W. Rogers, editor of the newspaper, asserted, "The greatest earthly friend of the colored race has fallen by the same spirit that has so long oppressed and destroyed us. In giving us our liberty he has lost his own life."[32] The editor of the *Christian Recorder* told its readers, "By the death of PRESIDENT LINCOLN our country has lost a patriot, a statesman, yea, a leader. Humanity has lost a friend, and the colored man one not easily replaced."[33] On April 22,

1865, the *New Orleans Tribune* published a speech by Henry Baker, whom the editor called a "friend" of its readers. The Black speaker moaned that "heaven as well as earth seems to be dressed in the black garments of woe . . . and we, my friends, still deeper sorrow for the friend of the colored man."[34]

The white teacher Laura M. Towne of Pittsburgh attended a speech by William Lloyd Garrison in Charleston on April 15, 1865. The sad news had not yet reached the port city. She reminisced that "shouts and cheers went up for Lincoln from the freed people of Charleston, at the mention of his name."[35] Upon returning to the village of Saint Helena after attending the flag-raising ceremony at Fort Sumter, she found numerous Blacks there prostrated by grief. Towne recalled a man telling her, "Oh, I have lost a friend." She asked, "What Friend?" The man responded, "They call him Sam, Uncle Sam, the best friend I ever had." According to the *Liberator*, when Black Charlestonians learned about the assassination, they "sobbed in the streets, My God! My God! Our friend is gone."[36] From Charleston to Washington to Baltimore and beyond, Black people were dealing with the realization that their "friend" in the struggle was no longer available to lend a sympathetic ear.

The death of Lincoln was a shattering event for numerous white Southerners. His humility and forgiving nature led them to conclude that they had also lost a champion. When the Confederate general Joseph E. Johnston learned of the murder, he let it be known that "Mr. Lincoln was the best friend we had."[37] Susanna Gordon Waddell of Richmond warned her fellow Southerners that the assassination "is far from being desirable for us" and it appears "now to have been the worst thing that could have happened to us."[38] The fire-eater and native Texan Louis T. Wigfall, who served in the U.S. Senate and the Confederate Senate, regretted the crime that had taken place on the Potomac River. He told a group of rebel officers that the president's death "is the greatest misfortune that could have befallen the South at this time. I knew Abe Lincoln, and, with all his faults, he had a kind heart."[39] Many Southern newspapers echoed the sentiment that Booth's diabolical act had deprived the conquered states of a guardian. The editor of the *Richmond Whig*, an anti-secessionist newspaper, confessed that Lincoln was a "friend" of the Southern states. Calling the late president "our statesman," the journalist noted that he displayed "kindheartedness" toward the defeated Confederates. "Let it be said that the germ of Peace," the article concluded, "was planted by the hand of Abraham Lincoln."[40]

African Americans believed that, as their benefactor, Lincoln would provide them with land, educational opportunities, and political rights. The enslaved segment of the population saw the acquisition of land as a prerequisite to maintaining their freedom. One way in which the Lincoln administration demonstrated its concern for Black Southerners and poor whites was the creation of the Bureau of Refugees, Freedmen, and Abandoned Lands, commonly known as the Freedmen's Bureau, in March 1865. Blacks occasionally petitioned Lincoln through letters for help with necessities such as food, shelter, money, and protection from abusive whites. Lincoln played a central role in the lives of Black people as their deliverer, friend, and benefactor.[41]

Days after the assassination, a street corner in Louisville, Kentucky, was the scene of a large gathering of Black mourners. It was there, according to a reporter, that "the whole assembly, as by one impulse, kneeling down upon the bare ground . . . showed how deeply their hearts were wrung by the death of their truest friend and benefactor."[42] On the same day as the Louisville program, a large meeting took place at the African Methodist Episcopal Church in Bloomington, Illinois, to memorialize Lincoln. By unanimous vote, the attendees adopted a set of resolutions, one of which stated, "*Resolved*, That while in the death of President Lincoln, the nation has sustained a great and irreparable loss, we, as colored American citizens have lost a *tried friend*—A GREAT DELIVERER—A BENEFACTOR."[43]

Shortly after the president's death, a crowd of Black Washingtonians assembled at the Fifteenth Street Presbyterian Church to express their sorrow. The meeting proclaimed that they had lost their "benefactor," a man whose "honesty" was beyond reproach.[44]

A New Orleans newspaper published an editorial in honor of the sad occasion. The periodical moaned, "Brethren, we are mourning for a benefactor of our race. Sadness has taken hold of our hearts. No man can suppress his feelings at this hour of affliction."[45] One Black preacher proclaimed that Lincoln's influence as a helper extended beyond the boundary of the United States. He asserted that Lincoln "was the world's benefactor, Heaven's gift to mankind."[46]

In June 1865, a group of Black Philadelphians donated a little more than eight dollars to the Lincoln Monument Fund. In presenting the funds to Mayor Alexander Henry, they rhapsodized, "We hope that you will receive it as a token of our respect and high esteem for the name of the immortal ABRAHAM LINCOLN, which we will cherish as the greatest benefactor of his day." The Black devotees concluded their statement to the mayor by reminding future Americans not to forget the historical significance of Lincoln. "Generations yet unborn shall rise up to commemorate and to celebrate the lustre of the name, life, and death of that hero," the statement said, "who first conquered the foe, and then fell in the triumph of victory."[47] The small size of the financial contribution was in no way indicative of their overwhelming gratitude for the assassinated leader.

As Secretary Gideon Welles made his way from the Petersen House to the Executive Mansion on the morning of Lincoln's death, he noticed "several hundred colored people, mostly women and children, weeping and wailing their loss" on Pennsylvania Avenue. Welles confessed that they "did not appear to diminish through the whole of that cold, wet day; they seemed not to know what was to be their fate since their great benefactor was dead, and their hopeless grief affected me more than anything else, though strong and brave men wept when I met them."[48] Obviously, the shedding of tears was not reserved for women only.

African Americans turned up the volume in proclaiming Lincoln their father, friend, and benefactor during the mourning period. Across the country, from New York to California, they responded to the assassination by identifying with the president in a personal way. For many Black people, the death of Lincoln symbolized the loss of a father figure or a close friend. Well into the twentieth century, the homes of many African Americans contained a photograph of Abraham Lincoln, which was representative of the federal government that brought freedom and hope to the downtrodden race.

CHAPTER SIX

Lincoln as a Symbol

PRESIDENT ABRAHAM LINCOLN was the most visible symbol of the national government. It was not surprising that Americans looked to him for leadership and inspiration. Those in bondage were certain that Lincoln's election to the nation's highest office had bestowed on him an incontestable amount of authority. They believed that he possessed the power to bring about the destruction of the evil institution. Formerly enslaved people and white Americans, however, saw a different image of the federal government when looking through the same lens after the assassination.

For white Americans, the government was not brought down by the death of an individual. A white soldier from Ohio had no reservations about how the government operated after the loss of its chief. William M. Fisher of the 103rd Ohio Volunteer Infantry accurately concluded that the death of a political leader, even if that person were the president, could not bring down the institution of government. Writing from Raleigh, North Carolina, on April 27, 1865, to his brother in Wellington, Ohio, Fisher said, "I thank the founders of our Government that they so arranged affairs of State so that the death of no one of its members will stop it for one moment."[1] Just maybe, he was drawing on his knowledge of presidential history. The U.S. government had continued to function after the deaths of William Henry Harrison and Zachary Taylor while in office.

The relationship between the former captives and Lincoln was one of mutual respect. By the end of the war, he had come to accept citizens of color as part of the American family, not as people to be merely tolerated. Their well-being and protection were important to the president. People of color saw Lincoln and the federal government as an inseparable tandem. Therefore, it was not surprising that many believed that the government had died along with the president. Strangely, this was the intention of John Wilkes Booth, who was certain that by murdering Lincoln, he would cause the government to suffer a political death. Booth's miscalculation brought about apprehension and sorrow, not the downfall of the government.

Emancipated people were deeply concerned about a return to the plantation. Their "exaggerated anxiety" was real, because the possibility of legal reenslavement was more than a vapid threat.[2] After all, there was no provision in the U.S. Constitution for ending slavery. Because of Lincoln's role in their emancipation, freedpeople saw him as an enduring symbol of their freedom. A Black preacher in Cincinnati called Lincoln the "symbol of freedom and authority."[3] Lincoln's death produced confusion among the liberated race. Across the South, they were gripped with trepidation in the days and weeks after the assassination.

Although the promulgation of the Emancipation Proclamation had occurred more than two years before Lincoln's death, there was still a great deal of uncertainty among those who were once held in captivity, because of the widely held notion that they owed their freedom to the president. Union general James H. Wilson, who was a formidable cavalry leader, was in Alabama when he heard the news. Wilson recalled that "for days the trembling creatures could not be induced to leave the camps, and it was only slowly and with difficulty that they could be made to realize that their former masters were finally deprived of power over them."[4]

The white plantation superintendent and Philadelphian Thomas Edwin Ruggles was on Saint Helena Island when Lincoln's hour struck. He sent a letter to a friend recounting the mood of African Americans there. "The death of Lincoln," Ruggles reported, "was an awful blow to the negroes here." He found them worried about the future of the federal government. He heard one say, "The Government is dead, isn't it? You have got to go North and Secesh [secessionists] come back, have n't you?" With a bit of paternalism, Ruggles said, "They could not comprehend the matter at all—how Lincoln could die and the Government still live. It made them very quiet for a few days."[5] He pointed to their lack of understanding about political democracy as the source of their confusion. Their limited experience with freedom and even less with democracy foretold of the challenges awaiting them.

The educator Elizabeth Hyde Botume remembered Jack Flowers, a former enslaved person who reflected on what the death of Lincoln meant to the newly minted freedpeople. Flowers believed that Lincoln's death had invalidated their freedom. He said, "I 'spect it's no use to be here. I might as well stayed where I was. It 'pears we can't be free, nohow. The rebs won't let us alone. If they can't kill us, they'll kill all our friens', sure."[6] Reverend Wallace Shelton tried to comfort former bondmen by reassuring them that the Almighty was on their side. He counseled, "God will see to it that the wicked do not triumph over us, and that we are not carried back into captivity."[7]

The noted Civil War nurse Clara Barton found herself near Andersonville prison as the conflict ended. By then, the nurse was attracting large numbers of people to her camp, many of whom were Black. African Americans traveled long distances to see "Miss Clara" because of her reputation for dealing honestly and truthfully with them. And indeed, Blacks wanted to know from her the facts about their leader's death and their status as freedpeople. Some whites had insisted that, on Lincoln's death, formerly enslaved people would be returned to bondage. The liberated captives were relieved when Barton informed them that they were still free.[8]

In Memphis, the New Hampshire native and chaplain of the Twenty-Seventh Ohio Regiment Colonel John Eaton was there when the end came for Lincoln. As the superintendent of freedmen for the Department of Tennessee and Arkansas, he had earned the trust of Blacks in the city. Eaton visited a Black church to gauge the members' attitude toward Confederate sympathizers. Upon entering the place of worship, he found that the "congregation . . . had concentrated itself into little groups of men, women and children, each group the center of a whirlwind of emotion." As Eaton walked the streets of Memphis, Blacks descended on him with questions about their freedom. "There was no more pathetic symbol of the loss the Nation suffered in that dark time," Eaton concluded, "than the distracted grief and bewilderment of these unhappy people."[9] The people Eaton encountered were overwrought and confused by the death of the president.

Lincoln was the emblem of peace and the spokesperson of ordinary people during the war. From the outset of the conflict, he knew that the nation would need to be made whole again. That process began when he issued the Reconstruction plan in December 1863. The ease with which the conquered Southerners could regain their place in the political family was compelling evidence that he was not guided by hatred or vindictiveness. "Lincoln represented a moral ideal," one scholar has suggested, "to which we all should aspire."[10]

Perhaps no document evidenced Lincoln's sentiment of peace more forcefully than his second inaugural address, in which he said, "with malice toward none; with charity for all." Lincoln concluded that famous oration by calling for "a just, and a lasting peace."[11] With General Robert E. Lee's surrender fresh in Lincoln's mind, he delivered the last speech of his life on April 11, 1865. Going forward, the president's hope for the country was "a righteous and speedy peace." After the war, Lincoln had come to symbolize peace and reunion. Under the president's blueprint for reconstructing the nation, the secessionists were invited to rejoin the Union with little resistance. Once they had agreed to a few stipulations, such as acknowledging the abolition of slavery and taking the oath of loyalty to the United States, they would be welcomed back into the political family.

A retrospective look at Lincoln's death reveals that it "served as a symbolic propitiation for the evil he had conquered" and as "an image of forgiveness."[12] One of the most significant moments of the Civil War was the collapse of the Confederate government at Richmond, which brought death to slavery itself. The collapse of the planters' archaic economic system signaled to the nations of the world that the United States had finally emerged from the darkness of slavery. One of the remarkable aspects of the postwar period was that the freedmen did not seek retribution against those who were responsible for their enslavement.

Lincoln believed that all Americans, regardless of race, deserved to be treated with dignity and respect. He knew that these human niceties were not extended to the slave population by the planter class. During the war, Lincoln reached the conclusion that the Constitution had to be amended if freedom were to be meaningful and permanent in the nation. He believed that the foundation of the American government was the Declaration of Independence, which announced not only that "all men are created equal" but also that they had a right to "life, liberty, and the pursuit of happiness."[13] This idea was not new. Lincoln had advanced it in a speech denouncing the *Dred Scott* decision in Springfield in June 1857. He argued that the inalienable rights enumerated in the Declaration of Independence applied "to all people of all colors everywhere."[14]

Lincoln understood that if the United States were to serve as a beacon of human rights to the world, the nation could not ignore the citizenship rights of people of African descent. As a universal symbol, Lincoln gave hope to untold numbers of poor and oppressed peoples. With the president's death, African Americans' most visible symbol of equality and racial justice was also gone.[15] Black people of the mid-nineteenth century had appropriated Lincoln as a symbol as a way of understanding the war, the government, emancipation, and the assassination. Lincoln, who had a hand in engineering the end of slavery, believed that freedom was a necessary antecedent for African Americans in pursuit of citizenship rights.

CHAPTER SEVEN

Campaigning for Full Citizenship Rights

A
FRICAN AMERICANS WERE forceful in their assertions
that equal justice was their birthright. The death of President Abraham Lincoln, however, made the climb to the
platform of social and political rights more difficult for them. In
addition to the military, the church as an institution occupied an
important place in the lives of citizens of color. Historically, the
Black church has been at the forefront of freedom movements in
the nation. African American clergy, the central figures in the
church, wielded tremendous power in their communities as religious leaders and political influencers.[1] The church was one of a
few places where Black people controlled their own affairs. African
American ministers, with their talents at organization and mobi-
lization, played an integral part in the movement for human rights.

As freedmen, Black Americans would have to navigate the
political waters of the post–Civil War era without Lincoln. In almost all the states along the Atlantic Ocean and in the North, and
to the California coast, Black citizens gathered in conventions to
issue statements confirming their devotion to Lincoln, and their
despair over their loss. One topic that was on the minds of Black
Americans was their attainment of civil rights, which Lincoln had
promised them, especially suffrage. The African Methodist Episcopal Church welcomed the meetings and conventions of activists
with open arms.

A week after the assassination, the African Methodist Episcopal
Church in Middleton, Connecticut, was the site of a public meeting to pay tribute to the president. One of the resolutions adopted

by the assembly expressed gratitude to Almighty God for supplying Lincoln with the courage and wisdom to "give peace to a suffering nation." Furthermore, the statement declared that Lincoln's "name and memory" would be cherished by people of African descent "as a martyr to our cause" for infinity.[2] The mournful crowd was convinced that John Wilkes Booth had robbed Black Americans of their most powerful ally in the struggle for citizenship.

The service of United States Colored Troops (USCT) to the nation was an important factor in persuading Lincoln to advance the idea of equal justice for people of color.[3] Black men enthusiastically had enrolled in the military with the hope of bettering their chance of acquiring civil rights and to demonstrate their manly qualities. The Ohioan Sergeant Robert A. Pinn of the Fifth USCT explained why he had volunteered to serve in the Union army. He claimed that the attack on Fort Sumter motivated him "to become a soldier, in order to prove by [his] feeble efforts the black man['s] rights to untrammeled manhood."[4] African American troops were determined not to disappoint their race, country, or commander in chief. The Black chaplain Chauncey Leonard believed that Lincoln had been the answer to their lack of equal justice. "We have looked to him as our earthly Pilot," he said of the president, "to guide us through this National Storm and Plant us Securely on the Platform of Liberty and Equal Political right."[5] Leonard believed that when the war was over, African Americans would be standing at the gate of citizenship rights. One of the most cherished events in Leonard's life was the meeting he, along with the educator George W. Samson, had with Lincoln on November 12, 1862. The two men discussed with the president how they could help to advance his colonization scheme.[6]

No doubt Corporal Jack Cherry of the Thirty-Fifth USCT voiced the sentiment of his unit when he told the Black periodical the *Leader*, of Charleston, South Carolina, in 1865 that they had been "faithful" soldiers and "ought to be considered as men."[7] While camped near Petersburg, Sergeant William McConlin of the Twenty-Ninth USCT warned politicians that "the colored soldiers have fairly won our rights by loyalty and bravery—shall we obtain them! If they are refused now, we shall demand them."[8]

Reverend Henry Highland Garnet of Washington was a powerful advocate for the men of the Black regiments. He was the pastor of the Fifteenth Street Presbyterian Church, which was one of the most influential religious institutions in Washington during the second half of the nineteenth century. Days after Congress passed the Thirteenth Amendment, Reverend Garnet delivered a sermon in the U.S. House of Representatives. Lincoln had requested that Garnet be extended an invitation to speak. He was the first person of color to give a speech in the Capitol Building. Garnet told the nation that the soldiers of the USCT had been denied political rights although they were courageously serving in the war to put down the rebellion.[9]

Delegates to the Pennsylvania State Equal Rights League doubtless beamed with pride as they recounted the military performance of the USCT. Meeting for two days in August 1865, at Union Wesleyan Church in Harrisburg, the activists strained to understand how these men could be denied the opportunity to participate in the nation's political process. One resolution emphasized the role of Black soldiers in the Union effort while advocating for them to be granted suffrage. The statement affirmed, "*Resolved*, That the unswerving loyalty and patriotism of our colored soldiers and sailors, as evinced by their unsullied courage . . . demand for them an admission into the arena of true manhood and freedom by giving them the right to vote."[10] The implication was that the manhood of Black warriors would be incomplete without access to the ballot box.

The *Albany Evening Journal* was no less forceful than African Americans themselves in advocating for suffrage for the men of the USCT. "No true man will deny the right of suffrage to those who have fought for the country," the newspaper assured, "whether native or adopted, black or white." The editorial concluded that "the franchise is altogether inconsistent with the condition of Slavery, while it is altogether consistent with the condition of Freedom."[11] This sentiment had won the approval of Lincoln before his death.

Two months after Lincoln had been laid to rest, a delegation of African American men of Connecticut assembled at the African Methodist Episcopal Church on Sperry Street in New Haven. The conference opened with the attendees petitioning the State of Connecticut to grant them their citizenship rights. The convention recognized the men of the Black regiments by asserting, "We view with peculiar pride and admiration the part our fathers, brothers, and sons have borne in this war . . . as displayed in their indomitable courage and endurance in the many hard fought battles of Port Hudson, Fort Wagner, Olustee, Petersburg, Fort Fisher, and others."[12] By listing these engagements, the delegates were calling attention to the bravery of the volunteers of the USCT.

In June 1865, Black men issued a call for a public meeting at Gilfield Baptist Church on Perry Street in Petersburg to petition the State of Virginia for the right to vote. The activists vowed, "We, the colored citizens of Petersburg, Va., and true and loyal citizens of the United States of America, claim, as an unqualified right . . . equality of rights under the law." To strengthen their appeal, the delegates offered a constitutional argument as a basis for equality. "Our color or former enslavement is no just cause for our proscription nor disfranchisement," the resolution said, "as the word white, nor slave, is not found in the Constitution of the United States."[13]

One way in which the formerly enslaved responded to Confederate defeat was to establish all-Black communities under the supervision of the Union army. These communities gave African Americans an opportunity to engage in the politics of governing. All-Black towns were places where the residents found camaraderie, protection, educational and employment opportunities, and cultural stability. By war's end, there were many African American villages and towns scattered throughout the South. One of the best known was Mitchelville, a town of three thousand inhabitants on Hilton Head Island. In the words of the *Liberator*, the leaders of Mitchelville conducted "their own affairs in a very creditable manner."[14]

On April 21, 1865, at a meeting of the Council of Administration, the governing body of the town, the officials drafted a set of resolutions in memory of Lincoln. The preamble to the resolutions stated that the assassination had seriously affected "the well-being of the nation, and in an especial manner the best interests of the colored people, from whose neck of bondage has been so recently removed, through the promptings of his truly Christian heart, would improve the occasion for giving utterance to the sad feelings which seek expression in this hour of deep affliction." The first formal statement offered by the distraught formerly enslaved people said, "Resolved, That we, the representatives of Mitchelville, look upon the Death of the Chief Magistrate of our country as a national calamity, and an irrepressible loss beyond the power of words to express." The members of the council reported that they would not allow their displeasure with the Confederates to degenerate into violence. They announced, "We will not mar this moment of our solemn sadness by encouraging feelings of vindicative revenge, but leave them to Him who doeth all things well, and has said, Vengeance is mine, I will repay."[15]

The assumption of leadership roles by Black men gave them a taste of political democracy and the motivation to continue the fight for human rights. This was one way of paying tribute to Lincoln. As shown at Mitchelville, Black people proved that they could grasp the fundamentals of politics and were capable of self-government when given a chance. Being in control, African Americans learned leadership skills that they would rely on when they moved on to larger government entities as they eventually did.

Sansom Street Hall in Philadelphia was the setting of a meeting under the direction of the Social, Civil, and Statistical Association of the colored citizens of Pennsylvania on July 17, 1865. The attendees invoked the name of Abraham Lincoln and recalled the service of Black men in the U.S. Army. Isiah C. Wears, who occupied the president's chair, stated that the purpose of the assembly was to advocate for suffrage for African Americans of Pennsylvania and across the nation. Before the meeting's close, the participants adopted the following statement: "WHEREAS, Union men, foremost in defending the country and the ever to be honored President, Abraham Lincoln, together with the Proclamation of Freedom, were unqualified in their declarations, that the cause of the war should cease with the war."[16] The delegates were categorical in their pronouncement that the preservation of the Union could not have been achieved without military victory.

Against the backdrop of Booth's crime, the editors of the *Black Republican* implored the federal government to grant African Americans equal rights. "We now want our rights as citizens," they wrote, "the privilege of the ballot box, to put in office those we know to be true to the flag of our country, and also to the friends of freedom." The editors warned that "the blood of our brave soldiers who have fallen upon the field in the defense of our country will cry out against this Government, and the wrath of a just God will continue to fall upon this once glorious and happy country."[17]

After the war, African American troops themselves appealed to state legislatures and the federal government to remove the obstacles blocking their path to political advancement. An illustration of this was the Sixtieth USCT, originally organized as the Iowa African First and mustered into service in October 1863. Six months after Lincoln's assassination, they met in convention at Davenport to appeal to their state to give them their human rights. The October 31, 1865, Convention of Colored Soldiers drafted several resolutions, one of which called on Iowa to amend its state constitution to allow Black troops the right to vote. The African American veterans bolstered their petition for suffrage by offering the following resolution: "We have discharged our duty as soldiers in the defense of our country" and therefore "ought to be trusted with the ballot." The delegates then stated that "the great work which God" selected for Lincoln "to perform has been so nearly accomplished that the wrath of the oppressor is utterly powerless to prevent a full and glorious consummation."[18] The Black soldiers believed that by connecting Lincoln to their struggle, they would prod the Iowa legislature into action on their behalf.

Seven months after the assassination, the Colored People's Convention of the State of South Carolina met at Zion Presbyterian Church in Charleston. For one year, black drapes decorated Zion, serving as a constant reminder to the members of what had happened to Lincoln. Black South Carolinians from all over the state met in Charleston in November 1865. The delegates issued an "Address to the Legislature of the State of SC" in which they voiced their opposition to the exclusion of African Americans from voting and the egregious Black Codes. The convention passed a set of resolutions to highlight a spirit of goodwill and cooperation among the races. One of the formal propositions extended an olive branch to the old planter class by referencing Lincoln's statement, "with malice toward none, with charity for all." The delegates wrote, "*Resolved*: That as the old institution of slavery has passed away, we cherish in our hearts no malice or hatred towards those who have held our brethren as slaves; but that we extend the right hand of fellowship to all, and make it our special aim to establish unity, peace, and love among all men."[19]

Black Georgians were just as active as people of color in other states in calling for their rights. The city of Augusta was the location of the Freedmen's Convention of Georgia in January 1866. The Black crusaders assembled at Springfield Baptist Church to press for political, social, and economic equality and to speak out against invidious treatment at the hands of white Georgians. It was the resolute opinion of the Committee of the Death of Mr. Lincoln "that if President Lincoln had lived, justice to all men irrespective of color, would have been meted out, and that the father of liberty would have been the father of rights."[20] The State of Georgia was unkind not only to African Americans but to Lincoln as well. Angered by the start of the war, citizens of Savannah hanged the president in effigy in 1861. After four years of fighting, there were examples of defeated Southern soldiers who were well behaved. Writing from Corpus Christi, Texas, to his brother on September 4, 1865, William Trail Jr. of Indiana, a member of the Twenty-Eighth USCT, told him that the remaining Confederates there were "perfectly sivel."[21]

The Convention of the Colored People of Tennessee opened its four-day meeting on August 7, 1865, in St. John's Chapel of the African Methodist Episcopal Church in Nashville. From all over the state 165 delegates arrived at the church to appeal to the Tennessee legislature to give them their citizenship rights. The delegates petitioned the state for the right to vote, fair wages, educational opportunities, and equal treatment before the law.[22] A little more than five hundred miles from Nashville, the National Equal Rights League convened its inaugural meeting in Cleveland, Ohio. The Oberlin College graduate and attorney John Mercer Langston occupied the president's chair during the three-day conclave in October 1865. The delegates pledged to continue a campaign of agitation until Black Americans were the beneficiaries of equality and suffrage.

On October 27, 1865, Reverend John J. Moore of San Francisco addressed the California State Convention of the Colored Citizens at Bethel African Methodist Episcopal Church on Seventh Street in Sacramento. Moore was born on a plantation in Virginia but escaped to the North, eventually settling in Boston. In the 1850s, he relocated to San Francisco, where he founded the first African Methodist Episcopal Zion Church in that city.[23] Reverend Moore implored the State of California to grant its Black citizens the right to vote as a lasting tribute to Lincoln. The Black preacher said, "We appeal to every true American whose voice shall resound in the proud capital over which the glorious stars and stripes shall float, to give us our rights in the name and spirit of the murdered and immortal Lincoln, who sealed our rights with his hallowed blood."[24]

African Americans in the state of Maryland also actively campaigned for their rights in an organized manner once the war had ended. Maryland was a slave state that remained loyal to the Union during the conflict. The State Colored Convention of Maryland met in Baltimore in December 1865 to crusade for equality and to speak for the Black citizens of the state with a collective voice. Bishop Alexander W. Wayman was elected president of the convention of approximately 155 delegates from across the state. Black citizens of Baltimore had an affinity for Lincoln. When the funeral train stopped there, African Americans turned out by the thousands to say goodbye. On December 29, the convention passed resolutions regarding the death of Lincoln, including the following:

"*Be it resolved*, That the exalted public and private character of the late President, his freedom from selfish ambition, his fear of God, his devotion to the eternal principles of liberty and justice . . . will cause his memory to be cherished" in perpetuity.[25]

African Americans in Illinois were also vocal in demanding their political rights. Galesburg, in the northwestern section of the state, was the location of a convention of Black men. The city was the place of the sixth debate between Stephen A. Douglas and Lincoln during the most famous senatorial campaign in the nation's history. Toward the end of the three-day meeting in October 1866, the fifty-six delegates issued the "Address of the Illinois Convention of Colored Men to the American People." The message asserted that it was Lincoln's wish that the federal government would grant suffrage to African American men. A portion of the public statement proclaimed the following: "A voice from the tomb of the martyred Lincoln seems now to reach the national ear, saying, 'The hour is come in which to enfranchise the colored American people.'"[26]

Campaigns for full citizenship rights and protests of inequality were national in scope. By protesting, Blacks were carrying on an American tradition that had roots in the colonial era of the 1770s. The self-advocates, however, were unable to force white politicians to grant African Americans full equality before the law. The failure of Black conventions was not due to a lack of organization or the inability of the leaders to articulate their grievances. Despite the invocation of Lincoln's name, racial oppression, especially by white Southerners, was too deeply entrenched for the Black crusaders to overcome. A letter to the *Christian Recorder* conveyed the belief of many African Americans regarding their denial of suffrage. The disgruntled writer said, "If the blacks of the South are denied the elective franchise, the war has failed to accomplish anything except a gigantic national debt, for black men to help pay."[27]

It was Lincoln's intention that equal rights for African Americans would coincide with the restoration of the Union. Black people anticipated the day when political and social equality would no longer be out of their reach. Although Lincoln did not live to see national Black suffrage become a reality, he had used his powerful and influential voice to call attention to the nation's long history of racial injustice. He acknowledged that opportunities for achievement or advancement should be available to all races.

A few years after the conflict, African American men enjoyed a measure of political success with the passage of the Reconstruction Act of 1867, which provided for adult male suffrage. Ex-Confederates who had been stripped of political power because of their participation in the war were denied this privilege. For the first time, African American men en masse would have the right to exercise voting privileges. This bold experiment did not give Black Southerners a permanent foothold in American democracy. It did not take long for them to realize that the franchise was not a panacea. The permanency of the nation after Appomattox and beyond depended heavily on Black people enjoying the benefits of American citizenship.

The conventions on several occasions made it clear that Lincoln's death was a significant loss not only to Black people but also to the nation. The conclaves revealed the affection that ordinary people of color and Black elites had for Lincoln. The numerous resolutions promulgated by Blacks were compelling testimony of the esteem in which they held the martyred chief. African Americans did not reject the support of sympathetic whites in their quest for human rights. Lincoln, formerly enslaved people, and Radical abolitionists hoped that Union victory would unlock the door to equal opportunity for citizens of color. The Union triumphed; however, it would take a hundred years after Lincoln's death and a great deal of social upheaval before Black Southerners were granted their full citizenship rights by the states and the federal government.

CHAPTER EIGHT

Johnson and Black Americans' Winter of Discontent

THE SOCIAL, POLITICAL, AND economic future of African Americans after the war rested in the hands of Andrew Johnson. The native of North Carolina felt the sting of poverty during his formative years. In search of a better life, he relocated to Greeneville, Tennessee, at the age of eighteen. In addition to political success in his adopted state, Johnson also acquired land and slaves, the two most prized possessions of white Southerners. Because of his support for the Union, President Abraham Lincoln appointed him the military governor of Tennessee in March 1862. Two years later Johnson, a Democrat, was Lincoln's running mate in the presidential election of 1864. Lincoln placed a high premium on the Tennessean's loyalty to the federal government and the need to show that he valued unity in the country.

Neither Lincoln nor Republican bosses gave much thought to what kind of chief executive Johnson would make. During that time, vice presidents in general spent their tenure in office in obscurity. A few weeks after Johnson's inauguration as vice president, the tragedy of Lincoln's assassination catapulted him into the national spotlight. Starting on April 14, 1865, Republican leaders, Democrats, African Americans, Southerners, and others would find out what kind of president Johnson would make. He was then confronted with the responsibility of reuniting the nation, which included protecting the freedom of Black Americans.

Even before the tragic event, Johnson was cozying up to African Americans. His paternalism, combined with arrogance, led him to believe that he could assume the leadership of people of African descent. In October 1864, in his role as governor of Tennessee, Johnson delivered a speech to a Black audience in Nashville where he blamed the planter aristocracy for oppressing them. Johnson then sent the hopes of the crowd soaring when he declared, "I will indeed be your Moses, and lead you through the Red Sea of war and bondage to a fairer future of liberty and peace."[1] He had struck the right chord to a group of people who had experienced hardship and disappointment for many years.

Vice President Johnson was on the list to be assassinated on the night of April 14, 1865. Fortunately for him, George Atzerodt, his would-be attacker, lost his nerve and failed to execute his part of the deadly plot. The sentiment in the United States after Lincoln's death was that there was a need for greater protection for the president. As a result, Johnson was "constantly surrounded by armed men; an officer from the War Department, with a loaded Derringer in each pocket, and revolver and knife in his belt is on duty with him, day and night."[2]

Within hours after Lincoln's death, the federal government passed from one who was admired and baptized in revolutionary turbulence to one who was untried and untested. As historian Eric Foner has put it, unlike his predecessor as president, Johnson "seem[ed] to shrink, not grow, in the face of crisis."[3] Once he was in office, citizens of color were willing to give the new president a chance to burnish his credentials as a champion of civil and political rights. Days after John Wilkes Booth's deadly act, President Johnson met with a delegation of men from the Black civil rights organization the National Equal Rights League at the Treasury Building in Washington. John Mercer Langston, the leader of the group, came away from the session convinced that the welfare of Black people was in good presidential hands. Some African Americans believed that Johnson would take Lincoln's place like Joshua had succeeded Moses.

In the immediate aftermath of the Washington catastrophe, some Black Americans, Radical Republicans, and white Northerners were certain that Johnson would deal more harshly with the former

Confederates than his predecessor. The *Black Republican* opined that the new president "is much more of a radical than the lamented Lincoln was and less disposed to temper justice with mercy."[4] Some clergy were sure of this as well. Reverend Wallace Shelton was convinced that Johnson was the Heavenly Father's selection to lead the nation during the time of transition and challenge. He told the crowd at the African Zion Baptist Church that "God will make him the instrument of His vengeance. He will deal out retribution, and mete out justice, with a steady and even hand."[5] Reverend Joseph A. Prime roared, "Let us pray that the mantle of our beloved and lamented President may fall upon his successor. And let the prayers of all good men ascend to God for the thorough healing of the nation."[6] Reverend Prime hoped that Johnson would be Lincolnesque in his leadership of the country.

During the early weeks of Johnson's presidency, Black newspapers, organizations, and religious institutions offered to cooperate with him. The delegates to the annual meeting of the South Carolina Conference of the African Methodist Episcopal Church in May 1865 adopted a resolution in which they promised their full cooperation to the new president. Meeting at Zion Church, the largest and most famous Black worship house in Charleston, the conference drafted the following statement: "*Resolved*, That we pledge our comfort, homes, lives, and sacred honor, if need be, to the support of A. Johnson, and the Government of the United States."[7] A memorial service held at Israel African Methodist Episcopal Church in Washington during the mourning period did not forget about the person who then occupied the nation's highest office. The lamenters adopted a resolution in which they prayed to God that Lincoln's successor, "Mr. Johnson, may be endowed with wisdom to guide the state of affairs right, so as to soon bring about a restoration of peace, justice, liberty, and happiness in our much-distracted country."[8] Calling on Johnson to exercise "wisdom" in executing the duties of the presidency made it difficult for him to escape the long shadow of the martyred leader. The editors of the newspaper the *Leader*, stated that Johnson was the right man to restore the country based on "universal equality."[9] With Johnson in the presidential chair, many journalists believed that citizenship rights for people of color were within their reach.

The end of the war found the formerly enslaved victims of harsh treatment at the hands of angry white Southerners. Since racism could be perpetrated in many ways, Black people could not escape white prejudice. In June 1865, a group of Black men from Richmond went to the White House to deliver a petition to Johnson. They told him, "Our old masters have become our enemies, who seek not only to oppress our people, but to thwart the designs of the Federal Government and of benevolent Northern associations in our behalf." These residents of Richmond explained to Johnson that they were still wearing mourning ribbons "as truthful expressions" of their sorrow for Lincoln. To strengthen their appeal, the Virginians told the president that their faith in the Union and "its Chief Magistrate" remained steadfast.[10] From all indications, Johnson gave the delegation a cordial reception. The political significance of his interactions with people of color cannot be overlooked. He wanted to please the Radical faction of the Republican Party by paying attention to human rights for Black citizens. And he also believed that he could win the affection and admiration of African Americans as Lincoln had done.

On July 4, 1865, the Colored People's Educational Monument Association held a commemorative program in honor of the slain president in Washington, D.C. As he had done on other occasions, Johnson sought to ingratiate himself to Black people by permitting the celebration to take place on the White House lawn. The presiding officer of the event was John F. Cook of Washington, who had gained notoriety as an educator, businessman, and member of the five-man delegation who met with Lincoln at the White House in August 1862. At that meeting, Lincoln was unsuccessful in convincing the Black leaders to support his colonization plan. Among the thousands in attendance at the Educational Monument Association event were politicians, government workers, and military men. The day's program consisted of speeches and the reading of letters from prominent Americans. Senator Henry Wilson, a Radical Republican from Massachusetts, was impressed by Johnson's overtures to

An unidentified USCT soldier wearing a black mourning ribbon on his upper right arm (ca. 1863–65). LC-DIG-ppmsca-34365, Prints and Photographs Division, Library of Congress.

people of color. Wilson told the gathering that the president would follow in the footsteps of Lincoln and "complete the great work of emancipation and enfranchisement."[11]

The festive celebration would have been incomplete without hearing from Frederick Douglass. Cook read a letter from the activist, who called for "the immediate, complete, and universal enfranchisement of the colored people of the whole country." Douglass ended his correspondence with the warning "that the prophecy of 1776 will not be fulfilled till all men in America shall stand equal before the law."[12]

Shortly after receiving the news of Lincoln's death, members of the National Theological Institute for Colored Ministers gave Johnson a set of resolutions. The institute, headquartered in the nation's capital, was established in 1865 by a group of Baptists to prepare Black men to enter the ministry. In making the presentation, Reverend Edmund Turney told Johnson that the resolutions were "expressive of their grief at the death of the late President, and their gratitude at the emancipation wrought in connection with his administration." One of the statements declared that the delegation of preachers was happy that God had allowed them "to witness the events relating to the emancipation and elevation of the colored people of this country, which in our own grateful remembrance . . . will ever be inseparable from the name and acts of Abraham Lincoln." The last resolution adopted by the religious leaders affirmed that in addition to praying for Johnson, they would work to help create and promote "a wise and good and righteous government" for all Americans.[13]

In accepting the resolutions, Johnson aimed the arrow of paternalism and condescension at the heart of citizens of color. He painted a rosy portrait of the planter class and a dire picture of Black people. The president told the group that some Southern Blacks exhibited a friendly disposition toward their former captors and that the ruling class was deeply interested in their well-being. As he continued to lecture the delegation, he suggested that the emancipated people had an inclination "to become loafers." Johnson should have known that chattel slavery was the engine that drove the Southern economy for generations. The president's myopic view of freedom meant that African Americans had to provide labor to the planter class. The chief executive was doubtful that Black and white people could coexist in the country and suggested colonization as a possible solution to the race problem. They heard him say that Black people could improve their moral character by ending "open and notorious concubinage."[14] There was no mistake that Johnson addressed the delegation of Black ministers as if he were a paragon of righteousness.

It did not take long for Blacks to realize that their faith and confidence in Johnson had been seriously misplaced. Douglass's observation of the president led him to conclude that he was not the right man to occupy the nation's highest office. He was also convinced that under Johnson, Black Americans' winter of discontent had arrived. In the opinion of the prominent abolitionist, a double tragedy had befallen the country. Douglass argued that the death of Lincoln and the direction in which Johnson was leading the nation combined to create "an unspeakable Calamity" for Black people.[15] Beatings, killings, and intimidation at the hands of white supremacists occurred with regularity in rural communities and cities. With Johnson's tacit approval, Southern governments enacted Black Codes, which relegated freedpeople to a position little better than slavery.

Because of this, Johnson enjoyed a great deal of popularity among white Southerners, and they in turn accepted him as their spokesperson. In many instances, their views and his aligned on matters of race. It was crystal clear that Johnson believed that white people as a race were superior to those of African ancestry. Furthermore, his low opinion of Black people led him to conclude that the United States was a country for white men.

Black people, Radical Republicans, and Northerners were underwhelmed by Johnson's Proclamation of Amnesty of May 29, 1865. According to the plan, ex-Confederates who affirmed their allegiance to the United States and to maintaining the freedom of Black people would be eligible to receive amnesty and pardons. Upon meeting these conditions, they would be in line to reclaim their property, except for their chattel. As a way of punishing the planter class, Johnson stipulated that those Southerners with property valued at $20,000 or more would have to apply directly to him for pardons. The president handed out pardons to ex-Confederates like candy at a Christmas parade. Those who were expecting that he would distinguish himself as a conscientious and judicious leader were disappointed. Blacks found the exclusion of the vote particularly discouraging. The ease with which ex-Confederates could regain their citizenship rights under the Reconstruction plan left many in the Black community disillusioned.

In general, the nation agreed with Johnson's harsh stand against the leaders of the Confederate government and his sympathetic posture toward poor whites. The founding of racially motivated movements such as the Ku Klux Klan and other white supremacist groups after the Civil War portended evil for African Americans. As one scholar accurately observes, "It was good for the Negro that his faith in America had been strengthened. For there were trying times just ahead."[16] There is little doubt that the road to racial justice for Black people might have been less bumpy if Lincoln had lived and their expectations had been met.

When a Black contingent, which included Douglass, visited Johnson in February 1866, tension and condescension filled the air. Cordiality was nowhere to be found. After the meeting, Johnson reportedly devalued Douglass by claiming that he was "just like any [N-word]" who "would sooner cut a white man's throat than not."[17] This meeting was a stark contrast to Douglass's interactions with the sixteenth president. Lincoln's treatment of the renowned Black leader was always good-natured and respectful. Black people who met Lincoln remembered him as being considerate and thoughtful. In October 1864, the abolitionist and social reformer Sojourner Truth left her session with Lincoln at the White House with a new attitude of respect for him. "I am proud to say that I never was treated with more kindness and cordiality," the women's rights advocate said, "than I was by the great and good man Abraham Lincoln."[18] Less than six months later, Truth would be viewing the remains of the Civil War president.

An illustration of Abraham Lincoln with Sojourner Truth during
their October 1864 meeting at the White House. The social reformer
came away claiming that he was "the best President ever."
Courtesy of the Detroit Historical Society.

Despite Johnson's effort to ingratiate himself to African Americans, there was still uncertainty as to where he stood regarding the welfare of Blacks. Because of his concessions to white Southerners, an elderly African American asked, "Do you think Mr. Johnson will hold fast to what he [Lincoln] did, or will he forget us, and send us back to the hell we was in?"[19] Thereafter, the fears of the formerly enslaved proved not to be unfounded. The notion of a gradual reenslavement weighed heavily on the minds of emancipated people. Slavery was still legal in Kentucky and Delaware until the ratification of the Thirteenth Amendment in December 1865.

A ray of hope pierced the clouds of darkness for Blacks along the Atlantic seacoast from Charleston to Jacksonville, Florida, as the war wound down. On January 15, 1865, while in Beaufort, South Carolina, General William T. Sherman issued Special Field Orders No. 15. The revolutionary but controversial directive stipulated that the head of each Black family could settle on forty acres of plowable land. The occupants of the land would be granted possessory titles, though they could not own the land outright until Congress legalized the titles. In another decree, Sherman made mules available to the families that had settled on the plots. The hopes of the farmers were dashed when Johnson invalidated Sherman's special field orders by returning virtually all the land to their original owners.

In October 1865, a committee of Black men on Edisto Island in South Carolina appealed to Johnson to allow freedmen to remain on federal lands. They intimated to him that their hearts were heavy and "Painful" at the possibility that the planters who had "cheated and Oppressed" them for decades would be restored as landholders. The petitioners told Johnson that their "Late and beloved President" had guaranteed their freedom with the Emancipation Proclamation and the successful prosecution of the war.[20] In spite of their persuasive powers, they were unable to convince the president to rescind his decision. A white teacher on the Sea Islands of South Carolina witnessed the displacement of Black farmers from the land that they thought was rightfully theirs. She observed, "The people receive the rebels better than we expected, but the reason is that they believe Johnson is going to put them in their old masters' power again, and they feel that they must conciliate or be crushed. They no longer pray for the President—*our* President, as they use to call Lincoln—in the church. They keep an ominous silence and are very sad and troubled."[21] What played out in South Carolina was duplicated across the South. The lack of the opportunity for formerly enslaved people to become homesteaders set the stage for them to remain destitute for many years.

The connection between land ownership and economic independence was not lost on freedpeople. Turner Jacobs of Mississippi doubtless spoke for many African Americans when he expressed his disappointment at this unfulfilled expectation to an interviewer of the Federal Writers' Project. He declared, "We all thought [Lincoln] was a young Christ come to save us, cause he promise every [N-word] forty acres and a mule. We never did get dat mule or dose forty acres either, cepten by hard work but we all lakked him thought he was a great man."[22] Americans had cherished the tradition of land ownership ever since the founding of the nation. Therefore, any form of land distribution was bound to fail.

By juxtaposing Johnson to Lincoln, the latter's status among African Americans shined even brighter. To many people of color who compared the two presidents, Lincoln seemed unblemished.[23] The new chief resident of the White House had difficulty grasping the idea that the power of the federal government could be used to affect the lives of millions of Americans in a positive way. He believed that the granting of civil and political rights to African Americans was the responsibility of the states. According to his understanding of the Constitution, the federal government did not have the authority to coerce states to guarantee equality between the races.

Because of initial optimism, Black people gave Johnson the benefit of the doubt. They hoped that he would not only continue but expand on the progress made during Lincoln's years in office. Yet Johnson's racist ideology, contentious personality, and stubbornness earned him the scorn of Black people and Radical politicians. Unfortunately for African Americans, none of Lincoln's presidential aura had rubbed off on Johnson. Perhaps in an ideal world Lincoln's brilliance would have been transferable, but that was not in fact the case. Lincoln took his presidential greatness with him to the grave. History has judged Abraham Lincoln as our nation's greatest president and Andrew Johnson as one of the worst.

Conclusion

TWO DAYS AFTER Abraham Lincoln's assassination, Charlotte Scott came up with the idea of building a statue to him. She was born a slave on a Virginia plantation. To escape the war there, Scott's owner William Rucker relocated to Marietta, Ohio, and freed her in 1862. Scott was living in the home of Rucker when she heard about the infernal deed. She took Lincoln's death as a personal loss. Scott expressed her sorrow to Rucker's wife, telling her, "The colored people have lost their best friend on earth. Mr. Lincoln was our best friend, and I will give five dollars of my wages toward erecting a monument to his memory."[1] When she made the foundational contribution, she could not have imagined that her name would be tied to Lincoln's legacy for many decades. During the years after the assassination, Scott emerged as a symbol of generosity, selflessness, and emancipation in the Black community. A Washington newspaper memorialized her when she died in 1891. The journal declared that her "name, at one time, was doubtless upon the lips of every man and woman in the United States and is now read by the thousands who annually visit the Lincoln statue at Lincoln Park" in the nation's capital.[2]

Within days of Scott's donation, people of color had gone to work to raise funds to build the statue. An editorial in the *Christian Recorder* called on Black Americans to contribute money for the construction of the monument. In making its solicitation pitch, the newspaper said, "It is but just to the memory of the martyred hero that the colored Americans should do something to perpetuate the name of one who sacrificed" his life for the cause of freedom.[3]

When Major Martin R. Delany asked people of color to contribute one cent each for a national monument, the race eagerly responded. Over time, African Americans gave to a fund that eventually reached several thousand dollars. The fundraising effort was especially impressive because many of the contributors were not long removed from slavery and were impoverished.

The Western Sanitary Commission, headquartered in Saint Louis, Missouri, assumed the responsibility of collecting the funds for the construction of the Freedmen's National Memorial Monument. The commission was well known among African Americans because of its outstanding reputation of providing aid to desperate Black refugees of the Western Theater. Black people trusted James E. Yeatman, president of the commission, to protect their donations.

A memorable event of 1876 revealed that the historical connection between Lincoln and Black Americans still existed eleven years after his death. On April 14, a huge crowd gathered for the unveiling of the Freedmen's Monument in Lincoln Park. The occasion was momentous because of the many dignitaries in attendance, including President Ulysses S. Grant, who pulled the cord to unveil the sculpture. The program also included Douglass's keynote address, "Oration in Memory of Abraham Lincoln." Thunderous applause filled the air when the presiding officer, John Mercer Langston, introduced Douglass, who used the unveiling ceremony to examine Lincoln's presidential years. According to the historian James Oakes, the prolific speaker did not use the occasion to focus on "the statue's demeaning symbolism."[4] The source of Douglass's displeasure with the statue was its representation of the Black person in a subordinate position. The sculpture, the work of Thomas Ball, depicted Lincoln holding a copy of the Emancipation Proclamation in his right hand. In the design, Lincoln was standing over a Black man with a forlorn look kneeling at his feet. "It showed the Negro on his knee," Douglass later demurred, "when a more manly attitude would have been indicative of freedom."[5] Two months after the ceremony, a Black newspaper in Alexandria, Virginia, proclaimed that the Freedmen's Monument was "unsurpassed for beauty and grandeur."[6] The magnificent statue was a source of pride for people of color.

In a lengthy speech, Douglass offered a critical analysis of Lincoln as president, which included a summary of his shortcomings followed by a recounting of his achievements on the question of race. Historian David W. Blight maintains that Douglass's "speech assumed the tone of a requiem, tempered by modest celebration, restrained nationalism, and redemptive hope."[7] More than a decade earlier, he had eulogized Lincoln at Cooper Union in New York City. In that 1865 oration, Douglass asserted that Lincoln was "emphatically" the president of the Black man. At the Washington dedication, he presented a different view of Lincoln. He announced that "Abraham Lincoln was not, in the fullest sense of the word, either our man or our model. In his interests, in his associations, in his habits of thought, and in his prejudices, he was a white man. He was pre-eminently the white man's President, entirely devoted to the welfare of white men." As Douglass continued his assessment, the audience heard him say that Lincoln "was willing to pursue, recapture, and send back the fugitive to his master" and that African Americans were "at best his step-children."[8] An explanation of Douglass's critical view of Lincoln then may be found in the number of years that had passed since the president's death and the orator's dissatisfaction with how Reconstruction was turning out.[9] As Douglass later confirmed in his speech, his criticisms of Lincoln were not the whole story. Before bringing his address to a close, he added, "But dying as he did die, by the red hand of violence, killed, assassinated, taken off without warning, not because of personal hate—for no man who knew Abraham Lincoln could hate him—but because of his fidelity to union and liberty, he is doubly dear to us, and his memory will be precious forever."[10] As Douglass took his seat, the audience cheered his effort, and the benediction ended the ceremony. By the time of the unveiling, the affection that many Black Americans had for the man who "had become a white martyr for black freedom" remained strong.[11]

Shortly after the dedication, Douglass reflected on the monument in a letter published in the *National Republican* in Washing-

ton in 1876. Douglass was troubled that the statue had not done a
better job of communicating the story of emancipation. At the same
time, however, he realized the difficulty if not the impossibility of
designing a single monument that could recount the entirety of a
historical event. He declared that the Freedmen's Monument did
not "tell the whole truth, and perhaps no one monument could be
made to tell the whole truth of any subject which it might be designed to illustrate." The orator believed that those in bondage had
played a Herculean role in their own liberation. The famous
American also pointed out his preference for a statue. "What I want
to see before I die," Douglass wrote, "is a monument representing
the negro, not couchant on his knees like a four-footed animal, but
erect on his feet like a man."[12]

According to the Black Illinois attorney Nathan Kellog McGill,
as the dark clouds of uncertainty descended on America, Lincoln
"became more and more determined as the task seemed more im-
probable."[13] The Civil War gave rise to the Emancipation Proclamation. Motivated by political and military concerns, Lincoln
responded to those who were suffering in captivity by proclaiming
some of them free and, probably more important, expressing a desire
to weaken the Confederacy. The validation of emancipation would
not have happened without Union victory. Lincoln, the master politician, was able to achieve freedom for enslaved people in a way that
limited disapproval.

Lincoln lived during a time when the country was steeped in
"contradictions and inconsistencies." But, unlike many of his contemporaries, he was able to rise above some of "its most loathsome
characteristics."[14] Shortly after Lincoln's death, Governor John A.
Andrew of Massachusetts addressed the legislature of the state.
He told the lawmakers that Lincoln was "cheerful, patient and
without egotism, he regarded and treated himself as the servant of
the people."[15] The same Lincoln was also a skillful and gregarious
politician who was quick with jokes, some of which were
indelicate.

Many Americans, exhausted by years of fighting and dispirited
by the devastation, paused to reflect on whether it was all worth it

This Lincoln statue, titled "Freedmen's Monument," in Lincoln Park, Washington, D.C., was made possible with money donated by African Americans. It was unveiled on April 14, 1876. (Image cropped.)
Courtesy of the Indiana Historical Society.

for the nation to remain an organic whole. With the end of the war in sight, Caroline H. Gilman, author and enthusiastic supporter of the Confederate cause, revealed her sense of sadness caused by years of carnage. Writing to a friend on April 2, 1865, Gilman, who was from Charleston by way of Boston, intoned, "The thought that man, made in the image of God, would become the butcher of his fellows, that the Gospel should be an empty sound is depressing, crushing to the heart."[16] Seven days later, the truce agreed to by Robert E. Lee and Ulysses S. Grant at Appomattox Court House signaled to a war-weary nation that the cataclysmic event was over. Both civilians and soldiers were worn out by the military contest, and they looked forward to returning to a life of normality. A visible reminder that the North had bested the South was the widespread devastation that dotted the Southern landscape. The Old South of slavery and secession now belonged to the pages of history.

The spell-binding speaker William Lloyd Garrison's faith in America had been shaken but not destroyed after the assassination. The editor of the *Liberator* and the central figure of the abolitionist crusade was hopeful for better days ahead for the country's Black population. Although the South was an inhospitable place for the emancipated race, Garrison remained optimistic. Writing to his friend and fellow abolitionist Benjamin Chase of Boston after the war, he told him that "the nation, as such, is becoming more and more just to the colored race . . . inspite of all the evil machinations of their enemies."[17] Black Southerners who were unable to protect or defend themselves from angry whites endured their wrath for decades. The prejudicial treatment of Black Americans did not diminish their devotion to the nation.

The African American social activist James B. Martin of Cleveland, Ohio, relocated to Washington before the start of the war. Writing to the *Cleveland Morning Leader* in June 1865 to defend the fealty of citizens of color, he proclaimed that no group was "more loyal and patriotic, during the whole of the gigantic struggle for national supremacy," than people of color.[18] To Black citizens, the United States was their home, giving them a renewed sense of identity and attachment to the nation of their birth.

The death of Lincoln simultaneously produced guilt and sorrow among some ex-bondmen, causing them to believe that the president had been murdered because of his role in their freedom and his plan to provide them with economic support during the postwar years.[19] Walter Brooks of Arkansas was convinced that Lincoln's death occurred because he planned to remunerate enslaved people for their years of suffering. "They say Abraham Lincoln principally was killed," Brooks told his interviewer, "because he was going to pay this money to the ex-slaves and before they would permit it they killed him."[20] Guilt led a Black mourner to wish that she could have exchanged places with Lincoln. According to the recollection of Jane Swisshelm, she heard an elderly Black woman in Washington yelling, "My good President! My good President! I would rather have died myself! I would rather have given the babe from my bosom! Oh, Jesus! Oh, Jesus!"[21]

The sorrow that surrounded African Americans found expression in the ways in which they honored the president. Across the land, Blacks responded by offering personal, organizational, and institutional tributes. African Americans also attended memorial services, wrote letters of condolence to newspapers, and participated in the historic funeral. Their reactions also included shedding tears, wearing mourning badges, and hanging photographs of Lincoln in their homes. Nan Stewart was typical of many formerly enslaved people when it came to showing their affection for Lincoln. Stewart told an interviewer from the Works Progress Administration, "One ob [*sic*] my prized possessions is Abraham Lincoln's picture."[22]

The response of Black Americans to Lincoln's death, however, did not cease with his burial. The emblems of mourning remained with African Americans long after the Confederate armies had surrendered and the flag at the White House had returned to full staff. Months and years afterward, ordinary people and Black leaders reflected on the historical significance of Lincoln to their race and to the country through speeches and encomium resolutions. An editorial in the *Colored Tennessean* proclaimed that Lincoln's name "will ever beautify the pages of our nation's history."[23] Although people of color showered Lincoln with soaring testimonials after his death, the glow of his name lost some of its luster in the Black community as the tragic event became a distant memory.

At the time of Lincoln's death, Black people could take pride in the role they had played in the destruction of slavery. Furthermore, Union victory affirmed that their future was in the United States, not Africa or Central America. One of the lessons learned by African Americans during Lincoln's presidency was that their humanity was important to him. It is safe to say that Lincoln's character served as an inspiration to a variety of groups throughout the nation including Blacks, whites, the wealthy, and the poor. Lincoln's assassination and the national funeral united Black and white citizens, excluding former Confederates, in a common bond of mourning. The story of the reaction of people of color to the assassination adds another layer to the historical record of African Americans and Abraham Lincoln.

NOTES

BIBLIOGRAPHY

INDEX

NOTES

Preface

1. Silkenat and Barr, "'Serving the Lord,'" 76.

Introduction

1. Andrews, *Six Women's Slave Narratives*, 30–31.
2. *Christian Recorder*, April 29, 1865.
3. Hodes, *Mourning Lincoln*, 9–10.
4. Richard Fox, *Lincoln's Body*, 50–51.
5. Hodes, *Mourning Lincoln*, 195.
6. Manning, "Shifting Terrain of Attitudes," 35.
7. *Black Republican*, April 22, 1865.
8. White, *To Address You*, xxiv.
9. Lincoln, *Collected Works*, 6:407.
10. Quarles, *Negro in the Civil War*, 340, 345.
11. Medford, *Lincoln and Emancipation*, 101.
12. Silkenat and Barr, "'Serving the Lord,'" 76.
13. Hodes, "Lincoln's Black Mourners," 70.
14. John Washington, *They Knew Lincoln*, 85.
15. Quarles, *Lincoln and the Negro*, 239.
16. Ramold, "'We Should Have Killed,'" 31.
17. Richard Fox, *Lincoln's Body*, xiii–xiv, 86.
18. Purcell, *Spectacle of Grief*, 4.
19. Litwack, *Been in the Storm*, 527.
20. *Christian Recorder*, April 22, 1865.
21. Goldfield, *America Aflame*, 366.
22. Hodes, *Mourning Lincoln*, 63.
23. Quoted in Hord and Norman, *Knowing Him by Heart*, 165.
24. *Christian Recorder*, April 22, 1865.

25. Hodes, *Mourning Lincoln*, 62.
26. Hodes, "Lincoln's Black Mourners," 71.
27. Quoted in Manning, *Troubled Refuge*, 237.
28. Lincoln, *Collected Works*, 3:145–46.
29. White, *To Address You*, 1–2.
30. Cheek and Cheek, *John Mercer Langston*, 370.
31. Philip Foner and Walker, *Black State Conventions*, 1:256.
32. Philip Foner and Walker, 5–7.
33. Quoted in Medford, *Lincoln and Emancipation*, 28.
34. Davis, *Image of Lincoln*, 153.
35. Quoted in Burlingame, *Black Man's President*, 18.
36. Stephens, *Voice of Thunder*, 12–13.
37. Lincoln, *Collected Works*, 4:250.
38. Douglass, *Life and Writings*, 3:72.
39. Quoted in McPherson, *Negro's Civil War*, 42.
40. Quoted in McPherson, 47.
41. Cheek and Cheek, *John Mercer Langston*, 387.
42. Ripley, *Black Abolitionist Papers*, 5:155.
43. Quoted in Blight, *Frederick Douglass' Civil War*, 139.
44. Rawick, *American Slave*, 7:293–94.
45. Rawick, 2:36.
46. Silkenat and Barr, "'Serving the Lord,'" 84.
47. Rawick, *American Slave*, 7:211.
48. Rawick, 14:361–62.
49. Levine, *Failed Promise*, 69.
50. Quoted in Berry and Blassingame, *Long Memory*, 148.
51. *Christian Recorder*, September 27, 1862.
52. Steiner, *Lincoln and Citizenship*, 57.
53. Quoted in Steiner, 96.
54. White, *To Address You*, 40.
55. Bennett, *Forced into Glory*, 465.
56. Quoted in White, *To Address You*, 54.
57. White, 55.
58. Burton, *Age of Lincoln*, 238.
59. *New Orleans Tribune*, April 15, 1864.
60. Manning, "Shifting Terrain of Attitudes," 19.
61. Quoted in White, *House Built by Slaves*, 136–38.
62. *New Orleans Tribune*, November 18, 1864.

1. Pandemonium on the Potomac River

1. Donald, *Lincoln*, 575.

2. Chester, *Thomas Morris Chester*, 277.

3. George A. Huron, "Personal Recollections of Abraham Lincoln," n.d., George Andrew Huron Papers, Manuscripts Collection, Box 1, Kansas Historical Society, Topeka, KS.

4. August V. Kautz to My Dear Mrs. Savage, April 3, 1865, August Kautz Papers, Manuscript Collection, Abraham Lincoln Presidential Library, Springfield, IL.

5. Sam S. Gardian to Adjutant General, April 13, 1865, Record Group 94, M619, R357, Letters Received by the Adjutant General's Office, 1861–1870, National Archives and Records Administration, Washington, DC.

6. *Christian Recorder*, April 22, 1865.

7. Reynolds, *Abe*, 883.

8. *Weekly Anglo-African*, May 13, 1865.

9. Newton, *Out of the Briars*, 19, 31, 32, 65, 66, 67.

10. Writers' Program, Virginia, *Negro in Virginia*, 213.

11. *Liberator*, April 28, 1865.

12. Michael Shiner Diary, Papers of Michael Shiner, 1813–1865, n.d., Reel 1, microfilm, Manuscript Division, Library of Congress, Washington, DC.

13. *Albany Evening Journal*, April 10, 1865.

14. *Liberator*, May 5, 1865.

15. *Liberator*, May 5, 1865.

16. Hine and Thompson, *Shining Thread of Hope*, 134–35.

17. Keckley, *Behind the Scenes*, 178.

18. Keckley, 178.

19. Lincoln, *Collected Works*, 8:399.

20. Lincoln, 8:403.

21. Horton and Horton, *Man and the Martyr*, 28.

22. Quoted in Winkle, *Lincoln's Citadel*, 413.

23. White, *House Built by Slaves*, 66–69.

24. Lincoln, *Collected Works*, 7:101. The Wadsworth letter did not appear in the press until after Lincoln's assassination. The original does not appear to have survived.

25. Quoted in White, *To Address You*, 235.

26. Holzer, *President Is Shot*, 62.
27. Donald, *Lincoln*, 588.
28. Rosen, *Confederate Charleston*, 153.
29. Lincoln, *Collected Works*, 4:240–41.
30. Keckley, *Behind the Scenes*, 137–38.
31. Donald, *Lincoln*, 593.
32. Hubbard and Nichols, "Contributions of Bernhardt Wall," 58.
33. Frederick L. Black, "Warned of Assassination, Lincoln Dreamed of It," February 6, 1926, Lincoln's Premonitions of Death Collection, Chicago Historical Society.
34. "Days of Bereavement," Lincoln's Scrapbook: News Clippings on Death and Funeral, 1865–1866, 139, Abraham Lincoln Presidential Library, Springfield, IL.
35. Wyatt-Brown, "Psychology of Hatred," 286.
36. Entry for April 14, 1865, Isham N. Haynie Diary, April 1865–July–August 1895, Isham N. Haynie Papers, Folder 3, Manuscript Collection, Abraham Lincoln Presidential Library, Springfield, IL.
37. U.S. War Department, *War of the Rebellion*, vol. 46, ser. 1, pt. 3, p. 781.
38. Welles, *Civil War Diary*, 628.
39. Quoted in Oates, *Abraham Lincoln*, 161.
40. Neill, "Reminiscences of the Last Years," 26, 31, 37.
41. *New Orleans Tribune*, April 21, 1865.
42. Davis E. Castle Journals, 1864–1865, April 15, 1865, James S. Schoff Civil War Collection, Box 1, Vol. 2, William L. Clements Library, University of Michigan, Ann Arbor, MI.
43. William H. Jones to Dear Sarah, May 2, 1865, American Historical Manuscripts, Box 6, Special Collections and Archives, Kent State University Libraries, Kent, OH.
44. "An Attempt to Describe the Future of the United States, 1863–1865," June 14, 1865, DAR.1937.06, Darlington Collection, Box 1, Folder 2, Special Collections Department, University of Pittsburgh, Pittsburgh, PA.
45. Union League draft resolution upon the death of Abraham Lincoln, April 1865, Ms 43938, Connecticut Museum of Culture and History, Hartford, CT.
46. Brown, *Negro in the American Rebellion*, 326.
47. Quarles, *Negro in the Civil War*, 345.
48. Hodes, *Mourning Lincoln*, 53.

49. Bishop, *Day Lincoln Was Shot*, 258.
50. Yellin, *Harriet Jacobs Family Papers*, 2:627, 630, 672.
51. Welles, *Civil War Diary*, 631.
52. *New York Herald*, April 20, 1865.
53. *New York Tribune*, April 19, 1865.
54. Quoted in White, *House Built by Slaves*, 187.
55. Keckley, *Behind the Scenes*, 191.
56. White, "They Saw Lincoln," 12.
57. Quoted in Coddington, *African American Faces*, 225–26.
58. *New York Tribune*, April 25, 1865.
59. Ellison, *True Mary Todd Lincoln*, 77.
60. Dirck, *Black Heavens*, 31.
61. Sorisio, "Unmasking the Genteel Performer," 32.
62. Writers' Program, Virginia, *Negro in Virginia*, 213–14.
63. Searcher, *Farewell to Lincoln*, 47.
64. *Elevator*, April 21, 1865, Black Abolitionist Archive, University of Detroit-Mercy.
65. U.S. War Department, *War of the Rebellion*, vol. 46, ser. 1, pt. 3, p. 797.
66. Trudeau, *Like Men of War*, 433–34.
67. *Chicago Tribune*, April 20, 1865.
68. Hewett, *Supplement to the Official Records*, 573.
69. *New York Tribune*, April 20, 1865.
70. John Washington, *They Knew Lincoln*, 157–58.
71. *New Orleans Tribune*, April 28, 1865.
72. *Liberator*, May 5, 1865.
73. Staudenras, *Mr. Lincoln's Washington*, 457.
74. Searcher, *Farewell to Lincoln*, 80–81.
75. Margaret Washington, *Sojourner Truth's America*, 322.
76. Pitch, *"They Have Killed Papa Dead!,"* 229–30.
77. John Washington, *They Knew Lincoln*, 159.

2. Slow Ride to Springfield

1. Holzer and the New-York Historical Society, *Civil War in 50 Objects*, 324.
2. Laderman, *Sacred Remains*, 158.
3. Searcher, *Farewell to Lincoln*, 93.
4. U.S. War Department, *War of the Rebellion*, ser. 1, vol. 46, pt. 3, p. 886.

5. E. D. Townsend to R. C. Drum, May 17, 1889, Record Group 94, M619, R327, Letters Received by the Adjutant General's Office, 1861–1870, National Archives and Records Administration, Washington, DC.

6. Arnold, *Life of Abraham Lincoln*, 436–37.

7. *Weekly Anglo-African*, April 22, 1865.

8. *New York Tribune*, April 25, 1865.

9. *Patriot and Union*, April 22, 1865.

10. Quarles, *Lincoln and the Negro*, 243.

11. *Daily National Intelligencer*, April 24, 1865.

12. Morris, *Memorial Record*, 164.

13. Emilie Davis Diaries, Collection 3030, April 15, 20, 22, and 24, 1865. Historical Society of Pennsylvania, Philadelphia, PA.

14. Richard Fox, *Lincoln's Body*, 85.

15. Valentine, *Obsequies of Abraham Lincoln*, 127.

16. Kunhardt and Kunhardt, *Twenty Days*, 15.

17. Holzer, *President Lincoln Assassinated!!*, 259.

18. Holzer, 260.

19. *New York Tribune*, April 25, 1865.

20. Ripley, *Black Abolitionist Papers*, 5:321–23.

21. Quoted in Burlingame, *Abraham Lincoln*, 2:824.

22. Quoted in Burlingame, 824.

23. *New York Tribune*, April 25, 1865.

24. Quoted in Searcher, *Farewell to Lincoln*, 139.

25. Valentine, *Obsequies of Abraham Lincoln*, 147.

26. Goggeshall, *Lincoln Memorial*, 179–89.

27. *New York Tribune*, April 25, 1865.

28. *Chicago Tribune*, May 2, 1865.

29. *New York Tribune*, April 25, 1865.

30. Sloan, "Abraham Lincoln's," 86.

31. Quoted in Holzer, *President Lincoln Assassinated!!*, 309.

32. Quoted in Holzer, 310.

33. Quoted in Holzer, 324.

34. Quoted in Holzer, 308–24.

35. *New York Times*, April 27, 1865.

36. Morris, *Memorial Record*, 182.

37. Quoted in Richard Fox, *Lincoln's Body*, 90.

38. Sherman's Address to His Army, May 30, 1865, Civil War Collection, Box 20, Folder 22, Stuart A. Rose Manuscript, Archives, and Rare Book Library, Emory University, Atlanta, GA.

39. Prince, *My Brother's Keeper*, 244.

40. Frost, *I've Got a Home*, 325.

41. Goggeshall, *Lincoln Memorial*, 222.

42. *Cleveland Morning Leader*, April 29, 1865.

43. *Weekly Anglo-African*, September 3, 1865.

44. Nicolay and Hay, *Abraham Lincoln*, 347.

45. *Chicago Tribune*, May 1, 1865.

46. *Daily Ohio Statesman*, May 1, 1865.

47. *Daily Ohio State Journal*, May 1, 1865.

48. Kunhardt and Kunhardt, *Twenty Days*, 223.

49. Trostel, *Lincoln Funeral Train*, 163.

50. Goggeshall, *Lincoln Memorial*, 265.

51. Goggeshall, 273–75.

52. *National Daily Intelligencer*, May 3, 1865.

53. *Chicago Tribune*, May 2, 1865.

54. *Christian Recorder*, May 20, 1865.

55. *Chicago Tribune*, May 2, 1865.

56. U.S. War Department, *War of the Rebellion*, ser. 1, vol. 46, pt. 3, p. 1081.

57. Quoted in White, *To Address You*, xvii–xix.

58. Quoted in White, xix.

59. Quarles, *Lincoln and the Negro*, 244.

60. Hannah, "Place in the Parade," 89.

3. The Emancipator and the Emancipated

1. Lincoln, *Collected Works*, 3:370.

2. Quoted in Bennett, *Forced into Glory*, 358.

3. Angell, *Bishop Henry McNeal Turner*, 41.

4. Ripley, *Black Abolitionist Papers*, 5:145.

5. Leonard, "Close Look," 93.

6. Lincoln, *Collected Works*, 7:243.

7. Kolchin, "Reexamining Southern Emancipation," 10.

8. Medford, *Lincoln and Emancipation*, 71.

9. Quoted in Hord and Norman, *Knowing Him by Heart*, 89.

10. Quoted in Hord and Norman, 90–91.

11. Rufus Saxton, "A Happy New Year's Greeting to the Colored People in the Department of the South," John Emory Bryant Scrapbook, 1861–1875, Box 11, William R. Perkins Library, Duke University, Durham, NC.

12. Yacovone, *Freedom's Journey*, 299.

13. Lincoln, *Collected Works*, 5:356–57.

14. Margaret Washington, *Sojourner Truth's America*, 423.

15. Engs, *Educating the Disfranchised*, 48.

16. Furness, "Negro as a Soldier," 457–58.

17. Meeting of Colored Soldiers and Sailors, n.d., Christian A. Fleetwood Papers, Manuscript Division, Library of Congress, Washington, DC.

18. Rawick, *American Slave*, 7:127.

19. Official Order of the Governor (John A. Andrew), March 23, 1863, Records of the Fifty-Fourth Massachusetts Infantry Regiment (Colored), 1863–1865, M1659, Roll 1, National Archives and Records Administration, Washington, DC.

20. Emilio, *Brave Black Regiment*, 308.

21. H. Northey Hooper to Brig General William Schouler Adjutant General State of Mass., April 27, 1865, The Negro in the Military Service of the United States, 1639–1886, M858, Roll 1, 141, Records of the Adjutant General's Office, Record Group 94, National Archives and Records Administration, Washington, DC.

22. *Christian Recorder*, May 27, 1865.

23. Edgar Dinsmore to My Dear Carrie, May 29, 1865, Edgar Dinsmore Papers, 1864–1865, William R. Perkins Library, Duke University, Durham, NC.

24. *Christian Recorder*, May 6, 1865.

25. *Christian Recorder*, May 6, 1865.

26. Andrews, *Six Women's Slave Narratives*, 3, 35.

27. Califf, *Record of the Services*, 70–71.

28. Solon to My Own Precious Wifey, April 18, 1865, Solon A. Carter Papers, Archives Branch, United States Army Heritage and Education Center, Carlisle Barracks, PA.

29. Warren Goodale to Dear Children, April 15, 1865, Warren Goodale Papers, 1847–1892, Massachusetts Historical Society, Boston, MA.

30. Carter, "Fourteen Months' Service," 179.

31. Quoted in Blassingame, *Slave Testimony*, 549.

32. Myers, "Black Women," 562.

33. Gannon, *Won Cause*, 162.
34. Rawick, *American Slave*, 8:113.
35. Guelzo, "How Abe Lincoln Lost," 7.
36. Taylor, *Embattled Freedom*, 214.
37. Medford, *Lincoln and Emancipation*, 77.
38. Margaret Washington, *Sojourner Truth's America*, 322.
39. George A. Huron, "Personal Recollections of Abraham Lincoln," n.d. George Andrew Huron Papers, Box 1, Kansas Historical Society, Topeka, KS.
40. Lincoln, *This Fiery Trial*, 87–88.
41. Burlingame, *Abraham Lincoln*, 2:831.
42. Prime, "Sermon Preached," 156.
43. *New York Tribune*, May 8, 1865.
44. *Albany Evening Journal*, April 26, 1865.
45. *Christian Recorder*, April 29, 1865.
46. Philip Foner and Walker, *Proceedings of the Black State Conventions*, 1:203.
47. Ripley, *Black Abolitionist Papers*, 5:350.
48. Ayers and Nesbit, "Seeing Emancipation," 3.
49. Botume, *First Days*, 173–78.
50. Botume, 173–75.
51. White, *To Address You*, 228.

4. Their Earthly Moses

1. John Washington, *They Knew Lincoln*, 25.
2. *Christian Recorder*, April 22, 1865.
3. Quoted in Klingman, *Abraham Lincoln*, 88.
4. White, *To Address You*, 230–31.
5. Barr, *Loathing Lincoln*, 49.
6. S. A. Morgan to Friend Charley, May 14, 1863, Charles Bennett Letters, 1862–1865, Folder 9, Historic New Orleans Collection, Williams Research Center, New Orleans, LA.
7. Carrie V. Still to Mr. White, November 25, 1864, Jacob C. White Papers, Moorland-Spingarn Research Center, Howard University, Washington, DC.
8. Dirck, *Black Heavens*, 46.
9. Thomas, "Sermon Preached," 45.

10. Prime, "Sermon Preached," 158.
11. Shelton, *Discourse upon the Death*, 5–6.
12. Quoted in Burton, *Age of Lincoln*, 237.
13. *Christian Recorder*, June 3, 1865.
14. *Christian Recorder*, May 27, 1865.
15. *Christian Recorder*, May 20, 1865.
16. Swisshelm, *Crusader and Feminist*, 287–88.
17. *Christian Recorder*, April 29, 1865.
18. Marrs, *Life and History*, 69.
19. *Christian Recorder*, May 6, 1865.
20. Quoted in Glatthaar, *Forged in Battle*, 207–8.
21. Quoted in Jenkins, *Climbing Up to Glory*, 98.
22. Keckley, *Behind the Scenes*, 190.
23. Jenkins, *Climbing Up to Glory*, 98.
24. Quoted in Silkenat and Barr, "'Serving the Lord,'" 79.
25. Hodes, *Mourning Lincoln*, 111.
26. White, *House Built by Slaves*, 160–63.
27. *Christian Recorder*, May 20, 1865.
28. Mary Ann Starkey to My Dear Friend, April 20, 1865, Edward W. Kinsley Papers, Department of Special Collections and University Archives, W. E. B. Du Bois Library, University of Massachusetts, Amherst, MA.
29. *Columbus Gazette*, April 21, 1865.
30. Thomas, "Sermon Preached," 46.
31. Shelton, *Discourse upon the Death*, 6.
32. Quoted in Hord and Norman, *Knowing Him by Heart*, 167–69.
33. Hill, *Sketch of the 29th Regiment*, 28.
34. Noyalas, "Civil War Institute Reveals," 18.
35. Thomas, "Sermon Preached," 46.
36. *Harper's Weekly*, May 13, 1865.
37. *Christian Recorder*, April 22, 1865.
38. *Black Republican*, April 29, 1865.
39. Andrews, *Six Women's Slave Narratives*, 58.
40. Blight, *Frederick Douglass*, 460.
41. Levine, *Failed Promise*, 45.
42. U.S. War Department, *War of the Rebellion*, ser. 3, vol. 3, p. 436.
43. Quoted in Quarles, *Lincoln and the Negro*, 245.
44. *Christian Recorder*, May 20, 1865.
45. *Black Republican*, April 22, 1865.

5. Father, Friend, and Benefactor

1. Lincoln, *Collected Works*, 7:23.
2. Reid Mitchell, *Vacant Chair*, 117.
3. Douglass, *Life and Writings*, 4:174.
4. *Weekly Anglo-African*, April 29, 1865.
5. Hodes, *Mourning Lincoln*, 116.
6. *Christian Recorder*, April 29, 1865.
7. Caroline Lewis, widow of John Lewis, September 8, 1877, WC 140665, Case Files of Approved Veterans Who Served in the Army and Navy in the Civil War and the War with Spain, 1861–1934, Records of the Veterans Administration, Record Group 15, National Archives and Records Administration, Washington, D.C.
8. Shelton, *Discourse upon the Death*, 4.
9. Cecelski, *Fire of Freedom*, 1, 74.
10. Albert Rogall Civil War Diary, 1864–1865, February 21, 1865, Albert Rogall Papers, Ohio History Connection, microfilm edition, Columbus, OH.
11. Charles Fox, *Record of the Service*, 74.
12. Quoted in Burlingame, *Abraham Lincoln*, 2:820.
13. Charles Fox, *Record of the Service*, 74–75.
14. Joseph Mitchell, *Badge of Gallantry*, 143.
15. Charles to Sister Lucy, May 4, 1865, Griswold Family Papers, 1862–1865, David M. Rubenstein Rare Book and Manuscript Library, Duke University, Durham, NC.
16. Quoted in Glatthaar, *Forged in Battle*, 208–9.
17. *Christian Recorder*, April 22, 1865.
18. Burlingame, *Abraham Lincoln*, 2:833.
19. Quoted in Glatthaar, *Forged in Battle*, 209.
20. *Weekly Anglo-African*, May 27, 1865.
21. Morris, *Memorial Record*, 117.
22. *New York Times*, April 19, 1865.
23. *Weekly Anglo-African*, April 29, 1865.
24. *Weekly Anglo-African*, May 13, 1865.
25. White, *House Built by Slaves*, 186–87.
26. Redkey, *Grand Army*, 293–95.
27. *Christian Recorder*, May 20, 1865.
28. Thomas, "Sermon Preached," 47.
29. Prime, "Sermon Preached," 155.

30. Quoted in Hodes, *Mourning Lincoln*, 112.
31. *Weekly Anglo-African*, May 13, 1865.
32. *Black Republican*, April 22, 1865.
33. *Christian Recorder*, April 22, 1865.
34. *New Orleans Tribune*, April 22, 1865.
35. Towne, *Letters and Diary*, 159–62.
36. *Liberator*, May 5, 1865.
37. Quoted in Avlon, *Lincoln and the Fight*, 188.
38. Quoted in Harrell, *When the Bells Tolled*, 34.
39. Quoted in Abbott, "Southern Reaction," 113.
40. *Richmond Whig*, April 21, 1865.
41. White, *To Address You*, 6.
42. *New York Times*, April 30, 1865.
43. *Christian Recorder*, April 29, 1865.
44. Quoted in Morris, *Memorial Record*, 153.
45. *New Orleans Tribune*, April 22, 1865.
46. Prime, "Sermon Preached," 156–57.
47. *Christian Recorder*, June 10, 1865.
48. Welles, *Civil War Diary*, 629.

6. Lincoln as a Symbol

1. Fisher to brother, April 27, 1865, William M. Fisher Papers, Ohio History Connection, Columbus, OH.
2. Hodes, *Mourning Lincoln*, 218.
3. Shelton, *Discourse upon the Death*, 4.
4. Catton, *This Hallowed Ground*, 490–91.
5. Pearson, *Letters from Port Royal*, 310–11.
6. Botume, *First Days*, 178.
7. Shelton, *Discourse upon the Death*, 7.
8. Oates, *Woman of Valor*, 331.
9. Eaton, *Grant, Lincoln*, 233–35.
10. Peterson, *Lincoln in American Memory*, 173.
11. Lincoln, *This Fiery Trial*, 221.
12. Shattuck, *Shield and a Hiding Place*, 130–31.
13. Tullai, "Abraham Lincoln," 92.
14. Lincoln, *Collected Works*, 2:406.
15. Escott, *Paying Freedom's Price*, 109.

7. Campaigning for Full Citizenship Rights

1. Wesley, *Politics of Faith*, 190.
2. Quoted in Hord and Norman, *Knowing Him by Heart*, 158–59.
3. Burlingame, *Black Man's President*, 41–42.
4. Cooney, "I Was . . . Eager," 281.
5. Quoted in Glatthaar, *Forged in Battle*, 209.
6. White, *House Built by Slaves*, 48–49.
7. *Leader*, December 11, 1865.
8. *Weekly Anglo-African*, May 13, 1865.
9. Medford, *Lincoln and Emancipation*, 100.
10. Philip Foner and Walker, *Proceedings of the Black National and State Convention*, 1:145–46.
11. *Albany Evening Journal*, July 25, 1865.
12. Connecticut State Convention of Colored Men, *Proceedings*.
13. *Virginia News*, June 9, 1865, quoted in the *New York Tribune*, June 15, 1865.
14. *Liberator*, May 5, 1865.
15. *Liberator*, May 5, 1865.
16. *Christian Recorder*, July 22, 1865.
17. *Black Republican*, April 22, 1865.
18. Redkey, *Grand Army*, 293–95.
19. *Leader*, December 24, 1865.
20. Freedmen's Convention of Georgia, *Proceedings*.
21. William Trail Jr. to My Dear Brother, September 4, 1865, William Trail Correspondence, Indiana Historical Society, Indianapolis, IN.
22. *Colored Tennessean*, August 12, 1865.
23. Yacovone, *Freedom's Journey*, 305.
24. Philip Foner and Walker, *Proceedings of the Black State Conventions*, 2:190.
25. *Daily National Republican*, December 30, 1865.
26. Illinois State Convention of Colored Men, "Address of the Illinois Convention," 36.
27. *Christian Recorder*, July 8, 1865.

8. Johnson and Black Americans' Winter of Discontent

1. Quoted in Brown, *Negro in the American Rebellion*, 330.

2. "How the President Is Guarded," n.d., Abraham Lincoln Collected Papers, Folder 4, Western Reserve Historical Society, Cleveland, OH. See also *Cleveland Leader*, May 5, 1865.

3. Eric Foner, *Fiery Trial*, xx.

4. *Black Republican*, April 22, 1865.

5. Shelton, *Discourse upon the Death*, 6.

6. Prime, "Sermon Preached," 157.

7. *Christian Recorder*, June 3, 1865.

8. *Christian Recorder*, June 3, 1865.

9. *Leader*, October 21, 1865.

10. "African Americans in Richmond," 38–39.

11. Levine, *Failed Promise*, 71.

12. Philip Foner and Walker, *Proceedings of the Black State Conventions*, 1:12–14.

13. Morris, *Memorial Record*, 71–72. See also Wesley, *Politics of Faith*, 251.

14. Escott, *Black Suffrage*, 174.

15. Levine, *Failed Promise*, 81.

16. Quarles, *Negro in the Making*, 125.

17. Quoted in White, *To Address You*, 238.

18. Quoted in Painter, *Sojourner Truth*, 206.

19. *New York Tribune*, April 20, 1865.

20. Eric Foner, *Voices of Freedom*, 1:297–98.

21. Towne, *Letters and Diary*, 167.

22. Quoted in Schwartz, *Abraham Lincoln*, 86.

23. Manning, "Shifting Terrain," 37.

Conclusion

1. Quoted in Quarles, *Lincoln and the Negro*, 4.

2. Quoted in White, *House Built by Slaves*, 202.

3. *Christian Recorder*, May 13, 1865.

4. Oakes, *Radical and the Republican*, 266.

5. Quoted in Quarles, *Negro in the Making*, 12.

6. White, *House Built by Slaves*, 200.

7. Blight, *Frederick Douglass*, 5.

8. Douglass, *Life and Writings*, 4:312.

9. Follett, Foner, and Johnson, *Slavery's Ghost*, 31.

10. Douglass, *Life and Writings*, 4:319.

11. Horton and Horton, *Man and the Martyr*, 36.

12. White and Sandage, "What Frederick Douglass Had."

13. Nathan Kellog McGill, "An Eulogy of Abraham Lincoln," 1909, Lincolniana Collection, Abraham Lincoln Presidential Library, Springfield, IL.

14. Medford, "Lincoln and African American Memory," 93.

15. John A. Andrew, "Message on the Death of Abraham Lincoln," April 17, 1865, John A. Andrew Collection, Chicago Historical Society, Chicago, IL.

16. Caroline Gilman to My Dear Friend, April 2, 1865, Caroline Howard Gilman Papers, 1810–1880, South Carolina Historical Society, Charleston, SC.

17. W. Lloyd Garrison to Benjamin Chase, July 24, 1865, African American History Collection, 1729–1970, Box 4, William L. Clements Library, University of Michigan, Ann Arbor, MI.

18. *Cleveland Morning Leader*, June 24, 1865.

19. Barr, "African American Memory," 156.

20. Rawick, *American Slave*, 8:257.

21. Swisshelm, *Crusader and Feminist*, 287–88.

22. Quoted in Silkenat and Barr, "'Serving the Lord,'" 82.

23. *Colored Tennessean*, October 7, 1865.

Manuscript Collections

Abraham Lincoln Presidential Library, Springfield, Illinois
  Isham N. Haynie Papers, Folder 3
  August Kautz Papers
  Lincoln's Scrapbook: News Clippings on Death and Funeral,
    1865–1866
  Lincolniana Collection
Black Abolitionist Archive, University of Detroit-Mercy, Detroit,
  Michigan
Chicago Historical Society, Chicago, Illinois
  John A. Andrew Collection
  Lincoln's Premonitions of Death Collection
Connecticut Museum of Culture and History, Hartford, Connecticut
  Manuscript 43938
Duke University, William R. Perkins Library, Durham, North
  Carolina
  John Emory Bryant Scrapbook, 1861–1875, Box 11
  Edgar Dinsmore Papers, 1864–1865
Duke University, David M. Rubenstein Rare Book and Manuscript
  Library, Durham, North Carolina
  Griswold Family Papers, 1862–1865
Emory University, Stuart A. Rose Manuscript, Archives, and Rare
  Book Library, Atlanta, Georgia
  Civil War Collection
Historical Society of Pennsylvania, Philadelphia, Pennsylvania
  Emilie Davis Diaries
Howard University, Moorland-Spingarn Research Center,
  Washington, DC
  Jacob C. White Papers
Indiana Historical Society, Indianapolis, Indiana
  William Trail Correspondence

Kansas Historical Society, Topeka, Kansas
    George Andrew Huron Papers, Box 1
Kent State University Libraries, Special Collections and Archives, Kent, Ohio
    American Historical Manuscripts, Box 6
Library of Congress, Manuscript Division, Washington, DC
    Christian A. Fleetwood Papers
    Papers of Michael Shiner, 1813–1865, microfilm
Massachusetts Historical Society, Boston, Massachusetts
    Warren Goodale Papers, 1847–1892
National Archives and Records Administration, Washington, DC
    Records of the Adjutant General's Office, Record Group 94
    Records of the Fifty-Fourth Massachusetts Infantry Regiment (Colored), 1863–1865
    Records of the Veterans Administration, Record Group 15
Ohio History Connection (formerly the Ohio Historical Society), Columbus, Ohio
    William M. Fisher Papers
    Albert Rogall Papers, 1864–1865, microfilm
South Carolina Historical Society, Charleston, South Carolina
    Caroline Howard Gilman Papers, 1810–1880
United States Army Heritage and Education Center, Carlisle Barracks, Pennsylvania
    Solon A. Carter Papers
University of Massachusetts, Department of Special Collections and University Archives, W. E. B. Du Bois Library, Amherst, Massachusetts
    Edward W. Kinsley Papers
University of Michigan, William L. Clements Library, Ann Arbor, Michigan
    African American History Collection
    Schoff Civil War Collection
    David E. Castle Journals, 1864–1865, Box 1
University of Pittsburgh, Special Collections Department, Pittsburgh, Pennsylvania
    Darlington Collection, Box 1, Folder 2
Western Reserve Historical Society, Cleveland, Ohio
    Abraham Lincoln Collected Papers, Folder 4

Williams Research Center, Historic New Orleans Collection, New
   Orleans, Louisiana
Charles Bennett Letters, 1862–1865, Folder 9

Newspapers

Albany (NY) Evening Journal
Black Republican (New
   Orleans)
Chicago Tribune
Christian Recorder
   (Philadelphia)
Cleveland Morning Leader
Colored Tennessean (Nashville)
Columbus Gazette
Daily National Intelligencer
   (Washington, DC)
Daily National Republican
   (Washington, DC)
Daily Ohio State Journal
Daily Ohio Statesman
Elevator (San Francisco)

Harper's Weekly (New York)
Leader (Charleston, SC)
Liberator (Boston)
National Daily Intelligencer
   (Washington, DC)
New Orleans Tribune
New York Herald
New York Times
New York Tribune
Patriot and Union (Harrisburg,
   PA)
Richmond Whig
Virginia News (Petersburg)
Weekly Anglo-African
   (New York)

Published Sources

Abbott, Martin. "Southern Reaction to Lincoln's Death." *Abraham
   Lincoln Quarterly* 7, no. 3 (September 1952): 111–27.
"African Americans in Richmond, Virginia, Petition President Andrew
   Johnson, 1865." In *Major Problems in African-American History*, vol. 2,
   From Freedom to "Freedom Now," 1865–1990s, Documents and Essays,
   edited by Thomas C. Holt and Elsa Barkley Brown, 38–39. Boston:
   Houghton Mifflin, 2000.
Andrews, William L. *Six Women's Slave Narratives*. New York: Oxford
   University Press, 1988.
Angell, Stephen Ward. *Bishop Henry McNeal Turner and African-
   American Religion in the South*. Knoxville: University of Tennessee
   Press, 1992.

Arnold, Isaac N. *The Life of Abraham Lincoln*. Introduction by James A. Rawley. Chicago: A. C. McClurg, 1884; repr., Lincoln: University of Nebraska Press, 1994.

Avlon, John. *Lincoln and the Fight for Peace*. New York: Simon and Schuster, 2017.

Ayers, Edward L., and Scott Nesbit. "Seeing Emancipation: Scale and Freedom in the American South." *Journal of the Civil War Era* 1, no. 1 (March 2011): 3–24.

Barr, John. "African American Memory and the Great Emancipator." In *Lincoln's Enduring Legacy: Perspectives from Great Thinkers, Great Leaders, and the American Experiment*, edited by Robert P. Watson, William D. Pederson, and Frank J. Williams, 133–64. Lanham, MD: Lexington Books, 2011.

———. *Loathing Lincoln: An American Tradition from the Civil War to the Present*. Baton Rouge: Louisiana State University Press, 2014.

Bennett, Lerone, Jr. *Forced into Glory: Abraham Lincoln's White Dream*. Chicago: Johnson, 2000.

Berry, Mary Frances, and John W. Blassingame. *Long Memory: The Black Experience in America*. New York: Oxford University Press, 1982.

Bishop, Jim. *The Day Lincoln Was Shot*. New York: Harper, 1955.

Blassingame, John W. *Slave Testimony: Two Centuries of Letters, Speeches, Interviews, and Autobiographies*. Baton Rouge: Louisiana State University Press, 1977.

Blight, David W. *Frederick Douglass' Civil War: Keeping Faith in Jubilee*. Baton Rouge: Louisiana State University Press, 1989.

———. *Frederick Douglass: Prophet of Freedom*. New York: Simon and Schuster, 2018.

Botume, Elizabeth Hyde. *First Days amongst the Contrabands*. Boston: Lee and Shepard, 1893; repr., New York: Arno Press and the New York Times, 1968.

Brown, William Wells. *The Negro in the American Rebellion: His Heroism and His Fidelity*. Boston: Lee and Shepard, 1867; repr., New York: Kraus Reprint, 1969.

Burlingame, Michael. *Abraham Lincoln: A Life*. 2 vols. Baltimore: Johns Hopkins University Press, 2008.

———. *The Black Man's President: Abraham Lincoln, African Americans, and the Pursuit of Racial Equality*. New York: Pegasus Books, 2021.

Burton, Orville Vernon. *The Age of Lincoln*. New York: Hill and Wang, 2007.

Califf, Joseph M. *Record of the Services of the Seventh Regiment, U. S. Colored Troops, from September 1863 to November 1866*. Providence: E. L. Freeman, 1878.

Carter, Solon A. "Fourteen Months' Service with Colored Troops." In *Civil War Papers: Read before the Commandery of the State of Massachusetts Military Order of the Loyal Legion of the United States*, 155–79. Wilmington, NC: Broadfoot, 1992.

Catton, Bruce. *This Hallowed Ground*. New York: Pocket Books, 1955.

Cecelski, Davis S. *The Fire of Freedom: Abraham Galloway and the Slaves' Civil War*. Chapel Hill: University of North Carolina Press, 2012.

Cheek, William, and Aimee Lee Cheek. *John Mercer Langston and the Fight for Black Freedom, 1829–1865*. Urbana: University of Illinois Press, 1989.

Chester, Thomas Morris. *Thomas Morris Chester, Black Civil War Correspondent: His Dispatches from the Virginia Front*. Edited by R. J. M. Blackett. Baton Rouge: Louisiana State University Press, 1989; repr., New York: Da Capo Paperback, 1991.

Coddington, Ronald S. *African American Faces of the Civil War: An Album*. Baltimore: Johns Hopkins University Press, 2012.

Connecticut State Convention of Colored Men. *Proceedings of the Conn. State Convention of Colored Men, Held at New Haven, June 6th and 7th 1865*. New Haven, CT: J. H. Benham, 1865. https://omeka.coloredconventions.org/items/show/1220.

Cooney, Charles F., ed. "I Was . . . Eager to Become a Soldier." By Robert A. Pinn. *Manuscripts* 26, no. 1 (Fall 1974): 280–82.

Davis, Michael. *The Image of Lincoln in the South*. Knoxville: University of Tennessee Press, 1971.

Dirck, Brian, R. *The Black Heavens: Abraham Lincoln and Death*. Carbondale: Southern Illinois University Press, 2019.

Donald, David Herbert. *Lincoln*. New York: Simon and Schuster, 1995.

Douglass, Frederick. *Life and Writings of Frederick Douglass*. Edited by Philip S. Foner. 5 vols. New York: International Publishers, 1950–55.

Eaton, John. *Grant, Lincoln, and the Freedmen: Reminiscences of the Civil War with Special Reference to the Work for the Contrabands and Freedmen of the Mississippi Valley*. In collaboration with Ethel Osgood Mason. New York: Longman's Green, 1907.

Ellison, Betty Boles. *The True Mary Todd Lincoln: A Biography.* Jefferson, NC: McFarland, 2014.

Emilio, Luis F. *A Brave Black Regiment: The History of the Fifty-Fourth Regiment of Massachusetts Volunteer Infantry, 1863–1865.* Boston: Boston Book, 1894.

Engs, Robert Francis. *Educating the Disfranchised and the Disinherited: Samuel Chapman Armstrong and Hampton Institute, 1839–1893.* Knoxville: University of Tennessee Press, 1999.

Escott, Paul D. *Black Suffrage: Lincoln's Last Goal.* Charlottesville: University of Virginia Press, 2022.

———. *Paying Freedom's Price: A History of African Americans in the Civil War.* Lanham, MD: Rowman and Littlefield, 2017.

Follet, Richard, Eric Foner, and Walter Johnson. *Slavery's Ghost: The Problem of Freedom in the Age of Emancipation.* Baltimore: Johns Hopkins University Press, 2011.

Foner, Eric. *The Fiery Trial: Abraham Lincoln and American Slavery.* New York: W. W. Norton, 2010.

———, ed. *Voices of Freedom: A Documentary History.* 3rd ed., 2 vols. New York: W. W. Norton, 2011.

Foner, Philip S., and George E. Walker, eds. *Proceedings of the Black National and State Conventions, 1865–1900.* 2 vols. Philadelphia: Temple University Press, 1986.

———, eds. *Proceedings of the Black State Conventions, 1840–1865.* 2 vols. Philadelphia: Temple University Press, 1979–80.

Fox, Charles Bernard. *Record of the Service of the Fifty-Fifth Regiment of Massachusetts Volunteer Infantry.* Salem, NH: Ayer, 1991.

Fox, Richard Wightman. *Lincoln's Body: A Cultural History.* New York: W. W. Norton, 2015.

Freedmen's Convention of Georgia. *Proceedings of the Freedmen's Convention of Georgia: Assembled at Augusta, January 10th, 1866, Containing Speeches of Gen'l Tillson, Capt. J. E. Bryant, and Others.* Augusta, GA: Loyal Georgian, 1866. https://omeka.colored conventions.org/items/show/524.

Frost, Karolyn Smardz. *I've Got a Home in Glory Land: A Lost Tale of the Underground Railroad.* New York: Farrar, Straus and Giroux, 2007.

Furness, William Eliot. "The Negro as a Soldier." In *Military Essays and Recollections, Papers Read before the Commandery of the State of Illinois, Military Order of the Loyal Legion of the United States,* 11:457–87. Wilmington, NC: Broadfoot, 1992.

Gannon, Barbara A. *The Won Cause: Black and White Comradeship in the Grand Army of the Republic.* Chapel Hill: University of North Carolina Press, 2011.

Glatthaar, Joseph T. *Forged in Battle: The Civil War Alliance of Black Soldiers and White Officers.* Baton Rouge: Louisiana State University Press, 1990.

Goggeshall, William T. *Lincoln Memorial: The Journeys of Abraham Lincoln: From Springfield to Washington, 1861, as President Elect, and from Washington to Springfield, 1865, as President Martyred.* Columbus: Ohio State Journal, 1865.

Goldfield, David. *America Aflame: How the Civil War Created a Nation.* New York: Bloomsbury, 2011.

Guelzo, Allen C. "How Abe Lincoln Lost the Black Vote: Lincoln and Emancipation in the African American Mind." *Journal of the Abraham Lincoln Association* 25, no. 1 (Winter 2004): 1–22.

Hannah, Eleanor L. "A Place in the Parade: Citizenship, Manhood, and African American Men in the Illinois National Guard, 1870–1917." In *Brothers to the Buffalo Soldiers: Perspectives on the African American Militia and Volunteers, 1865–1917,* edited by Bruce A. Glasrud, 86–111. Columbia: University of Missouri Press, 2011.

Harrell, Carolyn L. *When the Bells Tolled for Lincoln: Southern Reaction to the Assassination.* Macon, GA: Mercer University Press, 1997.

Hewett, Janet B., et al., eds. *Supplement to the Official Records of the Union and Confederate Armies.* 93 vols. Wilmington, NC: Broadfoot, 1994–98.

Hill, Isaac J. *A Sketch of the 29th Regiment Connecticut Colored Troops.* Microfiche ed. Baltimore: Daugherty, Maguire, 1867.

Hine, Darlene Clark, and Kathleen Thompson. *A Shining Thread of Hope: The History of Black Women in America.* New York: Broadway Books, 1998.

Hodes, Martha. "Lincoln's Black Mourners: Submerged Voices, Everyday Life, and the Question of Storytelling." *Social Text* 33, no. 125 (December 2015): 68–76.

———. *Mourning Lincoln.* New Haven, CT: Yale University Press, 2015.

Holzer, Harold. *The President Is Shot: The Assassination of Abraham Lincoln.* Honesdale, PA: Boyds Mills, 2004.

———, ed. *President Lincoln Assassinated!! The Firsthand Story of the Murder, Manhunt, Trial, and Mourning.* New York: Library of America, 2014.

Holzer, Harold, and the New-York Historical Society. *The Civil War in 50 Objects*. Introduction by Eric Foner. New York: Viking, 2013.

Hord, Fred Lee, and Matthew D. Norman, eds. *Knowing Him by Heart: African Americans on Abraham Lincoln*. Urbana: Knox College Lincoln Studies Center and University of Illinois Press, 2023.

Horton, James Oliver, and Lois E. Horton. *The Man and the Martyr: Abraham Lincoln in African American History and Memory*. 45th Annual Fortenbaugh Memorial Lecture. Gettysburg, PA: Gettysburg College Civil War Institute, 2006.

Hubbard, Charles M., and Chloe Nichols. "The Contributions of Bernhardt Wall and Edwin Markham to the Legacy of Abraham Lincoln." *Lincoln Herald* 106, no. 2 (Summer 2004): 56–64.

Illinois State Convention of Colored Men. "Address of the Illinois Convention of Colored Men to the American People." In *Proceedings of the Illinois State Convention of Colored Men, Assembled at Galesburg, October 16, 17, and 18, Containing the State and National Addresses Promulgated by It, with a List of the Delegates Composing It*, 1–37. Chicago: Church, Goodman, and Donnelley, Printers, 1867.

Jenkins, Wilbert L. *Climbing Up to Glory: A Short History of African Americans during the Civil War and Reconstruction*. Wilmington, DE: Scholarly Resources, 2002.

Keckley, Elizabeth. *Behind the Scenes; Or, Thirty Years a Slave and Four Years in the White House*. New York: G. W. Carlton, 1868; repr., New York: Oxford University Press, 1998.

Klingman, William K. *Abraham Lincoln and the Road to Emancipation, 1861–1865*. New York: Viking, 2001.

Kolchin, Peter. "Reexamining Southern Emancipation in Comparative Perspective." *Journal of Southern History* 81, no. 1 (February 2015): 7–40.

Kunhardt, Dorothy Meserve, and Philip B. Kunhardt Jr. *Twenty Days: A Narrative in Text and Pictures of the Assassination of Abraham Lincoln and the Twenty Days and Nights That Followed the Nation in Mourning, the Long Trip Home to Springfield*. Foreword by Bruce Catton. New York: Castle Books, 1965.

Laderman, Gary L. *The Sacred Remains: American Attitudes toward Death, 1799–1883*. New Haven, CT: Yale University Press, 1999.

Leonard, Ann. "Close Look at Lincoln's Words Shows Emancipator's Motives." *Lincoln Herald* 103, no. 2 (Summer 2001): 93–95.

Levine, Robert S. *The Failed Promise: Reconstruction, Frederick Douglass, and the Impeachment of Andrew Johnson.* New York: W. W. Norton, 2021.

Lincoln, Abraham. *The Collected Works of Abraham Lincoln.* Edited by Roy P. Basler. 9 vols. New Brunswick, NJ: Rutgers University Press, 1953–55.

———. *This Fiery Trial: The Speeches and Writings of Abraham Lincoln.* Edited by William E. Gienapp. New York: Oxford University Press, 2002.

Litwack, Leon F. *Been in the Storm So Long: The Aftermath of Slavery.* New York: Alfred A. Knopf, 1979.

Manning, Chandra. "The Shifting Terrain of Attitudes toward Abraham Lincoln and Emancipation." *Journal of the Abraham Lincoln Association* 34, no. 1 (Winter 2013): 18–39.

———. *Troubled Refuge: Struggling for Freedom in the Civil War.* New York: Alfred A. Knopf, 2016.

Marrs, Elijah P. *The Life and History of the Rev. Elijah P. Marrs.* Louisville, KY: Bradley and Gilbert, 1885; repr., Miami: Mnemosyne, 1969.

McPherson, James M. *The Negro's Civil War: How American Blacks Felt and Acted during the War for the Union.* New York: Vintage Civil War Library, 2003.

Medford, Edna Greene. "Lincoln and African American Memory." In *Lincoln Lessons: Reflections on America's Greatest Leader,* edited by Frank J. Williams and William D. Pederson, 91–100. Carbondale: Southern Illinois University Press, 2009.

———. *Lincoln and Emancipation.* Carbondale: Southern Illinois University Press, 2015.

Mitchell, Joseph B. *The Badge of Gallantry: Recollections of Civil War Congressional Medal of Honor Winners.* New York: Macmillan, 1986.

Mitchell, Reid. *The Vacant Chair: The Northern Soldier Leaves Home.* New York: Oxford University Press, 1993.

Morris, Benjamin F. *Memorial Record of the Nation's Tribute to Abraham Lincoln.* Washington, DC: W. H. and O. H. Morrison, 1865.

Myers, Amrita Chakrabarti. "Black Women, Religious Rhetoric, and the Legacy of Abraham Lincoln." *Journal of African American History* 94, no. 4 (Fall 2009): 561–70.

Neill, William D. "Reminiscences of the Last Years of President
    Lincoln's Life." In *Glimpses of the Struggle: A Series of Papers Read
    before the Minnesota Commandery of the Military Order of the Loyal
    Legion of the United States*, 29–53. Wilmington, NC: Broadfoot, 1992.

Newton, Alexander. *Out of the Briars: An Autobiography and Sketch of
    the Twenty-Ninth Regiment Connecticut Volunteers*. Philadelphia:
    A.M.E. Book Concern, 1910.

Nicolay, John, and John Hay. *Abraham Lincoln: A History*. New York:
    Century, 1890.

Noyalas, Jonathan A. "Civil War Institute Reveals Black Veteran's
    Thoughts about Lincoln." *Lincoln Forum Bulletin*, no. 53 (Spring
    2023): 18–19. https://www.thelincolnforum.org/the-lincoln-forum
    -bulletin.

Oakes, James. *The Radical and the Republican: Frederick Douglass,
    Abraham Lincoln, and the Triumph of Antislavery Politics*.
    New York: W. W. Norton, 2007.

Oates, Stephen B. *Abraham Lincoln: The Man behind the Myths*.
    New York: Harper and Row, 1984.

———. *A Woman of Valor: Clara Barton and the Civil War*. New York:
    Free Press, 1994.

Painter, Nell Irvin. *Sojourner Truth: A Life, a Symbol*. New York:
    W. W. Norton, 1996.

Pearson, Elizabeth Ware. *Letters from Port Royal: Written at the Time
    of the Civil War, 1862–1868*. Boston: W. B. Clarke, 1906; repr.,
    New York: Arno and the New York Times, 1969.

Peterson, Merrill D. *Lincoln in American Memory*. New York: Oxford
    University Press, 1994.

Pitch, Anthony S. *"They Have Killed Papa Dead!": The Road to Ford's
    Theatre, Abraham Lincoln's Murder, and the Rage for Vengeance*.
    Hanover, NH: Steerforth, 2008.

Prime, Joseph A. "Sermon Preached in the Liberty Street Presbyterian
    Church (Colored)." In *A Tribute of Respect by the Citizens of Troy, in
    the Memory of Abraham Lincoln*, 151–58. Albany, NY: J. Munsell,
    1865.

Prince, Bryan. *My Brother's Keeper: African Canadians and the
    American Civil War*. Toronto: Dundurn, 2015.

Purcell, Sarah J. *Spectacle of Grief: Public Funerals and Memory in the
    Civil War Era*. Chapel Hill: University of North Carolina Press,
    2022.

Quarles, Benjamin. *Lincoln and the Negro*. New York: Oxford University Press, 1962; repr., New York: Da Capo, 1991.

———. *The Negro in the Civil War*. Boston: Little, Brown, 1953.

———. *The Negro in the Making of America*. New York: Macmillan, 1969.

Ramold, Steven F. "'We Should Have Killed Them All': The Violent Reaction of Union Soldiers to the Assassination of Abraham Lincoln." *Journal of Illinois History* 10, no. 1 (Spring 2007): 27–48.

Rawick, George P., ed. *The American Slave: A Composite Autobiography*. 19 vols. Westport, CT: Greenwood, 1972.

Redkey, Edwin S., ed. *A Grand Army of Black Men: Letters from African-American Soldiers in the Union Army, 1861–1865*. New York: Cambridge University Press, 1992.

Reynolds, David S. *Abe: Abraham Lincoln in His Times*. New York: Penguin, 2020.

Ripley, C. Peter, ed. *The Black Abolitionist Papers*. 5 vols. Chapel Hill: University of North Carolina Press, 1987–91.

Rosen, Robert N. *Confederate Charleston: An Illustrated History of the City and the People during the Civil War*. Columbia: University of South Carolina Press, 1994.

Schwartz, Barry. *Abraham Lincoln and the Forge of National Memory*. Chicago: University of Chicago Press, 2000.

Searcher, Victor. *The Farewell to Lincoln*. New York: Abingdon, 1965.

Shattuck, Gardiner H., Jr. *A Shield and a Hiding Place: The Religious Life of the Civil War*. Macon, GA: Mercer University Press, 1987.

Shelton, Wallace. *A Discourse upon the Death of Abraham Lincoln, Late President of the United States, Delivered in Zion Baptist Church, Cincinnati*. Newport, KY: W. S. Bailey, 1865.

Silkenat, David, and John Barr. "'Serving the Lord and Abe Lincoln's Spirit': Lincoln and Memory in the WPA Narratives." *Lincoln Herald* 115, no. 2 (2013): 75–98.

Sloan, Richard E. "Abraham Lincoln's New York City Funeral." In *The Lincoln Assassination: Crime and Punishment, Myth and Memory*, edited by Harold Holzer, Craig L. Symonds, and Frank J. Williams, 55–93. New York: Fordham University Press, 2010.

Smith, John David. *Lincoln and the U.S. Colored Troops*. Carbondale: Southern Illinois University Press, 2013.

Sorisio, Carolyn. "Unmasking the Genteel Performer: Elizabeth Keckley's *Behind the Scenes* and the Politics of Public Wrath." *African American Review* 34, no. 1 (Spring 2000): 18–38.

Staudenras, P. J., ed. *Mr. Lincoln's Washington: The Civil War Dispatches of Noah Brooks.* South Brunswick, NJ: Thomas Yoseloff, 1967.

Steiner, Mark E. *Lincoln and Citizenship.* Carbondale: Southern Illinois University Press, 2021.

Stephens, George E. *A Voice of Thunder: The Civil War Letters of George E. Stephens.* Edited by Donald Yacovone. Urbana: University of Illinois Press, 1997.

Swisshelm, Jane Gray. *Crusader and Feminist: Letters of Jane Gray Swisshelm, 1858–1865.* Edited by Arthur J. Larsen. Saint Paul: Minnesota Historical Society, 1934.

Taylor, Amy Murrell. *Embattled Freedom: Journeys through the Civil War's Slave Refugee Camps.* Chapel Hill: University of North Carolina Press, 2018.

Thomas, Jacob. "Sermon Preached in the African Methodist Episcopal Zion Church." In *A Tribute of Respect by the Citizens of Troy, in the Memory of Abraham Lincoln*, 43–47. Albany, NY: J. Munsell, 1865.

Towne, Laura M. *Letters and Diary of Laura M. Towne, Written from the Sea Islands of South Carolina.* Edited by Rupert Sergent Holland. Cambridge, MA: Riverside, 1912.

Trostel, Scott D. *The Lincoln Funeral Train: The Final Journey and National Funeral for Abraham Lincoln.* Fletcher, OH: Cam-Tech, 2002.

Trudeau, Noah Andre. *Like Men of War: Black Troops in the Civil War, 1862–1865.* Boston: Little, Brown, 1998.

Tullai, Martin D. (Mitch). "Abraham Lincoln—Racist, Bigot or Misunderstood?" *Lincoln Herald* 103, no. 2 (Summer 2001): 85–92.

U.S. War Department. *The War of the Rebellion: A Compilation of the Official Records of the Union and Confederate Armies.* 128 vols. and index. Washington, DC: Government Printing Office, 1880–1901.

Valentine, David T. *Obsequies of Abraham Lincoln, in the City of New York.* New York: Edmund Jones, 1866.

Washington, John E. *They Knew Lincoln.* New York: E. P. Dutton, 1942.

Washington, Margaret. *Sojourner Truth's America.* Urbana: University of Illinois Press, 2009.

Welles, Gideon. *The Civil War Diary of Gideon Welles, Lincoln's Secretary of the Navy: The Original Manuscript Edition*. Edited by William E. Gienapp and Erica L. Gienapp. Urbana: Knox College Lincoln Studies Center and University of Illinois Press, 2014.

Wesley, Timothy L. *The Politics of Faith during the Civil War*. Baton Rouge: Louisiana State University Press, 2013.

White, Jonathan W. *A House Built by Slaves: African American Visitors to the Lincoln White House*. Lanham, MD: Rowman and Littlefield, 2022.

———, ed. "They Saw Lincoln: Two Black Army Doctors." *Lincoln Forum Bulletin*, no. 51 (Spring 2022): 12–13. https://www.thelincolnforum.org/the-lincoln-forum-bulletin.

———, ed. *To Address You as My Friend: African Americans' Letters to Abraham Lincoln*. Foreword by Edna Greene Medford. Chapel Hill: University of North Carolina Press, 2021.

White, Jonathan W., and Scott Sandage. "What Frederick Douglass Had to Say about Monuments." *Smithsonian Magazine*, June 30, 2020. https://smithsonianmag.com/history/what-frederick douglass-had-say-about-monuments-180975225/.

Winkle, Kenneth J. *Lincoln's Citadel: The Civil War in Washington, DC*. New York: W. W. Norton, 2013.

Writers' Program, Virginia. *The Negro in Virginia*. New York: Hastings House, 1940.

Wyatt-Brown, Bertram. "The Psychology of Hatred and the Ideology of Honor: Current Parallels in Booth's Lincoln Conspiracies." In *The Battlefield and Beyond: Essays on the American Civil War*, edited by Clayton E. Jewett, 265–90. Baton Rouge: Louisiana State University Press, 2012.

Yacovone, Donald, ed. *Freedom's Journey: African American Voices of the Civil War*. Chicago: Lawrence Hill Books, 2004.

Yellin, Jean Fagan, ed. *The Harriet Jacobs Family Papers*. 2 vols. Chapel Hill: University of North Carolina Press, 2008.

INDEX

Note: Italicized page numbers indicate figures.

Abbott, Anderson Ruffin (Black surgeon), 40

abolitionists, 11, 13, 15, 17, 19, 25. *See also* Douglas, Hezekiah Ford; Douglass, Frederick; Truth, Sojourner

"Address of the Illinois Convention of Colored Men to the American People," 121

African Methodist Episcopal Church, 14, 17, 53, 82, 105, 125; annual conference (1865), 23–24; eulogies for Lincoln in, 87–88; resolutions by, 113–14

Age of Lincoln, The (Burton), 18

Albany Evening Journal, 25, 115–16

Allen, Richard, 17

American Anti-Slavery Society (New York City), 53

American Colonization Society, 16–18

Anderson, Robert, 29–30, *31*

Andersonville prison (Georgia), 110

Andrew, John A., 75, 138

Anthony, William H. (clergy), 82

Arago (steamer), 29

Army of Northern Virginia, 24–25

Army of the James, Twenty-Fifth Corps, 23

Army of the Potomac, Twenty-Fourth and Twenty-Fifth Corps, 21

assassination of Lincoln, 1–2, 20, 24; anger at in North, 36; Baltimore plot, 30; Black criticisms ceased after, 36–37; Black refugees' reaction to, 80–81; Black troops' reaction to, 75–76; Black Washingtonians keep vigil at Petersen House, 35; Booth's blueprint for, 32–33; construction of casket platform, 39; Easter Sunday sermons, 86–87; effect on Black soldiers, 7, 48, 88–89, 100–103; Emancipation Proclamation as catalyst for, 72; fears of, 25–27; on Good Friday, 30, 93; as loss for country, 99; military commission of inquiry, 23; moment of, 33, *34*; sesquicentennial of, 6; Stanton's telegram to Dix, 33–35; as symbolic propitiation, 111–12; synonymous with losing a family member,

Leonne M. Hudson, associate professor emeritus at Kent State University, is the author of *The Odyssey of a Southerner: The Life and Times of Gustavus Woodson Smith* and the editor of *Company "A" Corps of Engineers, U.S.A., 1846–1848, in the Mexican War.* He coedited *Democracy and the American Civil War: Race and African Americans in the Nineteenth Century.*